Clothed with Christ

Wearing an Attractive Faith

William S. Bentley

VIDE

Copyright © 2020 by Vide Press

Vide Press and The Christian Post are not responsible for the writings, views, or other public expressions by the contributors inside of this book, and also any other public views or other public content written or expressed by the contributors outside of this book. The scanning, uploading, distribution of this book without permission is theft of the Copyright holder and of the contributors published in this book. Thank you for the support of our Copyright.

Vide Press
6200 Second Street
Washington D.C. 20011
www.VidePress.com

ISBN 978-1-7351814-4-8

Printed in the United States of America

Unless otherwise noted Scripture quotations are taken from the Holy Bible, New International Version®, NIV®. Copyright © 1973, 1978, 1984, 2011 by Biblica, Inc.™ Used by permission. All rights reserved worldwide.

Scripture quotations marked (CEV) are from the Contemporary English Version Copyright © 1991, 1992, 1995 by American Bible Society. Used by Permission.

Scripture quotations marked (ESV) are taken from The Holy Bible, English Standard Version®, copyright © 2001 by Crossway, a division of Good News Publishers. Used by permission. All rights reserved.

Scripture quotations marked (MSG) are taken from The Message. NavPress, 2002. Copyright © 1994, 1995, 1996, 2000, 2001, 2002. Used by permission of NavPress Publishing Group.

Clothed With Christ

We that have been saved
are clothed with Christ
coated by the example of the risen Lord,
who humbled himself
while here on earth
who walked in sandals
on the dusty roads,
who was without a home,
a migrant preacher
out in the wilderness
clothed with his worker's hands
to do the work he left
for us to complete,
to do greater than he
through the sands of time
until the new creation
each of us is destined to be

Raymond A. Foss

Table of Contents

Introduction: Clothed with Christ.................... 1

Chapter 1: **Muddy People**
(Our Basic Composition) 5

Chapter 2: **Nothing to Wear**
(Fig Leaves Optional?) 17

Chapter 3: **Clothes Make the Man**
(You Are What You Wear) 33

Chapter 4: **I Wouldn't Be Caught Dead in That**
(Fashion Faux Pas: What Not to Wear) 45

Chapter 5: **A Wolf in Sheep's Clothing**
(God Sees the Deception)................................ 55

Chapter 6: **Fashion: In One Year and Out the Other**
(Adapting to the Culture) 71

Chapter 7: **Dressed for Battle—Part One**
(This Means War!)....................................... 85

Chapter 8: **Dressed for Battle—Part Two**
(Outfitted Head to Toe) 105

Chapter 9: **In Your Glad Rags**
(Dressed for the Homecoming) 125

A(fter)word of Encouragement 145

Acknowledgments................................... 149

Notes 151

Introduction: Clothed with Christ

> Get out of bed and get dressed! Don't loiter and linger, waiting until the very last minute. Dress yourselves in Christ, and be up and about! (Romans 13:14, MSG)

> Consider then, O man! Whether there can be anything more wretched and poor, more naked and miserable, than man when he dies, if he be not clothed with Christ's righteousness, and enriched in his God. (Johann Arndt)

Perhaps you've had the experience of reading the Bible when a particular verse that you have read several times before suddenly leaps off the page, old words seen through new lenses. Why does this happen? Most often, our scripture reading assumes a "skimming" process—like driving down the interstate while failing to notice the beautiful field of sunflowers in the median. In doing so, we often fail to notice the important truths that God has "hidden in plain sight," until we have a spiritual revelation.

Brain scientists have referred to a similar phenomenon known as a *scotoma*. Scotomas are essentially mental "blind spots" that keep us from seeing truths that are right before us. For example, some of us (especially those of my vintage) are quite familiar with looking for a seemingly lost pair of glasses or a set of keys, only for someone to point out, *Why—they're right there in front of your nose*. How, you say, can something in plain view escape notice? You may even convince yourself that you looked in the exact spot of the so-called missing item, and it wasn't there a minute ago.

To give even further credence to this phenomenon, read the statement below and count the number of the letter "F":

FINISHED FILES ARE THE RESULT OF YEARS OF SCIENTIFIC STUDY COMBINED WITH THE EXPERIENCE OF MANY YEARS OF EXPERTS.

If you said there were two, you would be incorrect. Three? Wrong again. In fact, there are seven letter F's all together. (Hint: Did you forget the letter "F" in the word "of" occurring four times? It's okay—many people do.)

As seen in that example, the answer was right in front of you, yet you may have failed to see it. The most likely explanation for this is that the word "of"—a rather small, insignificant word—is one that our minds do not dwell on when reading because we are focused on the seemingly more "important" and longer words in the text. Over time, our brains have been trained to disregard smaller words as we read in order to grasp the most meaning from the least amount of text.

Similarly, we also gloss over daily encounters and situations that we have already decided are trivial or not important. In other words, we create beliefs based on experiences, learning opportunities, and perceptions that generate a particular mindset. We take this mental outlook with us and apply it to our daily encounters with people, situations, and information. The important takeaway from this is that what you believe or don't believe can hurt you[1] (or at the very least, leave you lacking in some capacity).

This also holds true in our regular reading of God's Word. If Bible study is seen as a destination rather than a journey (or a thing to be checked off a "to-do" list rather than a means of spiritual formation), then it's likely that we will often *hear* but not *recognize* or even *internalize* important truths God may be trying to convey to us through his Word. We allow *spiritual* scotomas to form that prevent or blind us to deeper spiritual truths at our disposal. As Eugene Peterson points out in his book *Eat This Book*, *how* we read the Bible is as important as *that* we read it.

> Eating a book takes it all in, assimilating it into the tissues of our lives. Readers become what they read. If Holy Scripture is to be something other than mere gossip about God, it must be internalized. . . . Words—spoken and listened to, written and read—are intended to do something *in* us, give health and wholeness, vitality and holiness, wisdom and hope. Yes, *eat* this book.[2]

Introduction: Clothed with Christ

Yet even those who "eat" the Bible regularly as their daily bread report having unique revelations from sections of Scripture or even a single verse that shed new meaning on the passage itself or personally applied to a life event. This is what happened to me several years ago while reading the book of Romans. In addressing the young gentile Christians in Rome, Paul exhorts them to lay claim to the light of their salvation by avoiding the dark deeds of the world:

> And do this, understanding the present time: The hour has already come for you to wake up from your slumber, because our salvation is nearer now than when we first believed. The night is nearly over; the day is almost here. So let us put aside the deeds of darkness and put on the armor of light. Let us behave decently, as in the daytime, not in carousing and drunkenness, not in sexual immorality and debauchery, not in dissension and jealousy. Rather, **clothe yourselves with the Lord Jesus Christ**, and do not think about how to gratify the desires of the flesh. (Romans 13:11–14, emphasis added)

It was on that particular reading that the words "clothe yourselves with the Lord Jesus Christ" nearly jumped off the page. In my casual, cursory reading of the Word, it was as if God had taken his holy highlighter and purposely caused those words to stand out. But it didn't just stop there. There were questions. What does that mean, to *clothe* yourself with Christ? How would that look? Would that mean emulating Jesus by wearing long flowing robes and sandals? Grow my gray beard longer? Or even more ludicrous, sling Jesus on my back like an old familiar sweater and "wear" him wherever I go?

In my reading and studying of Scripture in the years to follow, complemented by the wisdom of Godly authors and scholars and the guidance of the Holy Spirit in my thinking and reflection, I have come to an imperfect but purer sense of what it means to be clothed with Christ. In the process, pre-existing scotomas were removed, much like the scales that fell from the Apostle Paul's eyes upon his conversion experience. In the following pages, I invite you to follow me—a fellow traveler—as we navigate with a new set of eyes through uncharted waters for some and very familiar territory for others. Regardless of our level of spiritual transformation, we travel the same road, are given the same Spirit (God's divine GPS), and are provided with the same map and coordinates (God's Word).

During our journey, take note of the various themes and motifs related to clothing and dress throughout Scripture. Consider how these treatments of apparel might enhance your understanding of being *clothed with* or *putting on* Christ. Don't be afraid to use your senses along the way, especially the sense of sight and the use of the mind's eye to visualize the various themes and related imagery. Above all, keep a traveler's log of your journey, capturing new and vital insights along the way.

So, are you ready to embark on our excursion? If so, then let the journey begin.

Chapter 1:
Muddy People
(Our Basic Composition)

> Then the LORD God formed a man from the dust of the ground and breathed into his nostrils the breath of life, and the man became a living being. (Genesis 2:7)

> The Lord he thought he'd make a man—dem bones gonna rise again.
> Made him out of clay and sand—dem bones gonna rise again.[1] (Traditional song)

Dust ... ground ... earth ... dirt. It doesn't get much more basic than that. On the sixth day of creation, *terra firmus* became *epidermis*. The clay of the earth became a day of new birth. From *adamah* (Hebrew for ground) came *adam* (Hebrew for man). Like a potter shaping a lump of mud on a cosmic wheel, the Creator fashioned his most prized *objet d'art* up until that point. If creating the heavens and the earth, separating light from darkness, casting celestial bodies into orbit, and forming vegetation and creatures of every kind were not enough, God saved his masterpiece for last.

But why dirt? Why not whittle a human being from a majestic redwood or chisel man from granite? Why didn't God choose to forge the human race from a precious metal? Or simply clone an angel?

Perhaps it's to remind us that without God's divine stroke, we are nothing but the ground we walk on. Unless he breathed life into man (Genesis 2:7), we would be nothing but lifeless lumps of clay. And because human beings are created in the image of God (*Imago Dei*), we have the potential to rise above our earthly vestiges, leaving behind literal shells of ourselves and aspiring to a greater glory unbound by our clay trappings.

Yet, many of us choose to cling to our dusty origins. Yes, we are thankful to be created in God's image, to share in his character and his capacity for love, relationship, and creativity. We are humbled by the fact that God made us "a little lower than the angels" and "crowned [us] with glory and honor" (Psalm 8:5). And we may feel blessed that he made us "rulers over the works of [his] hands" and "put everything under [our] feet" (Psalm 8:6). Instead, we prefer to stay grounded in the normal, in the safety of that which is solid, loamy, and familiar.

If only we realized that we were made for much more than that.

Mud the Medium

So, back to the original question: Why dirt? Why mud? Interestingly, Jesus sometimes used mud to heal. As described in the Gospel of John, Jesus formed mud by spitting on the ground and forming a type of poultice to apply to the eyes of a man who had been blind from birth. The man, after washing the mud from his eyes in the Pool of Siloam, was given back his sight (John 9:1–7). No doubt, Jesus could have simply placed his hands on the man's eyes and said, "Be healed," with the same result. But for some reason, he chose dirt and saliva as the medium to restore the man's vision, possibly an outward symbol that he could use any method or resource at his disposal—even mud and spittle—to bring about transformation and life.

Muddy People

In the same way, Jesus can use our dirty, earthly shells to produce something good, to redeem his fallen creation, and to breathe life into lives that are dead or wasting away. Sometimes we fall into the trap of thinking that we need to be an elegantly made teapot, a fancy Ming vase, or an ornate sculpture. But God doesn't want museum pieces that merely sit on display to be admired. Rather, he made us to be practical and useful—to be functional in the sense of carrying out his kingdom on earth. If we serve God as he intended, our worship will be directed back to Him through our love and service to others who in turn will be drawn to the Creator, adding to the repository of vessels at his disposal.

Additionally, if we allow God to shape and mold us (like a potter reshaping his artwork), we will continue to be formed into the object that will best serve His purposes. We are reminded of this in Jeremiah 18:1-6 when the prophet is told by God to visit the local potter:

> This is the word that came to Jeremiah from the LORD: "Go down to the potter's house, and there I will give you my message." So I went down to the potter's house, and I saw him working at the wheel. But the pot he was shaping from the clay was marred in his hands; so the potter formed it into another pot, shaping it as seemed best to him. Then the word of the LORD came to me. He said, "Can I not do with you, Israel, as this potter does?" declares the LORD. "Like clay in the hand of the potter, so are you in my hand, Israel."

And in Romans 9:21:

> Does not the potter have the right to make out of the same lump of clay some pottery for special purposes and some for common use?

Obviously, God has total artistic freedom and control when it comes to fashioning our lives for his purposes. We only need to realize the function for which we have been designed. Should we fail to do so, the consequences are clear: God can destroy that which he has created if he sees fit. This was Job's concern:

Your hands shaped me and made me.
Will you now turn and destroy me?
Remember that you molded me like clay.
Will you now turn me to dust again? (Job 10:8–9)

The Error in Our Ways

As God's creations, we often err in one of two ways. For some, we are pieces of priceless art to be placed on the pedestal of human admiration, averting the glory due to God toward ourselves. Perhaps more troubling, though, is our penchant for trivializing or even criticizing God for the "vessels" he has created. Whether it be our physical appearance, our particular abilities or aptitudes (or perceived lack thereof), or our personalities, we never seem completely satisfied with the Maker's original blueprints or designs. Who hasn't mused, "If only I were taller, prettier, smarter, happier, more popular, etc."? Our laundry lists of grievances often sound more like spoiled children who don't get what they want for Christmas than the grateful recipients we should be. We are like the Israelites kvetching about their state of affairs in the wilderness rather than rejoicing over their freedom from bondage. But God (through the prophet Isaiah) makes it clear what He thinks of such protests:

> "Woe to those who quarrel with their Maker,
> those who are nothing but potsherds
> among the potsherds on the ground.
> Does the clay say to the potter,
> 'What are you making?'
> Does your work say,
> 'The potter has no hands'?
> Woe to the one who says to a father,
> 'What have you begotten?'
> or to a mother,
> 'What have you brought to birth?'

"This is what the LORD says—
the Holy One of Israel, and its Maker:
Concerning things to come,
do you question me about my children,
or give me orders about the work of my hands?
It is I who made the earth
and created mankind on it." (Isaiah 45:9–12)

Through a Glass Darkly

In essence, we have become our own idols as well as our own critics. We can't stop looking at ourselves in the mirror, either to fawn over or look away in disappointment. As for the latter, if God were to truly grant our wishes and give us the looks, personality, aptitudes, or gifts we desire, would we be finally satisfied? Or would some other fault, blemish, or inadequacy arise to ask, "If only . . . ?" No, we must come to realize that the loving Creator uniquely fashioned each of us for a specific purpose—and it's up to each of us to discover what that purpose is.

For others of us, we are satisfied simply to live uncomplicated lives, settling for a mediocre existence. We fail to appreciate God's glory, joy, and majesty in the commonplace. C. S. Lewis probably put it best:

> If we consider the unblushing promises of reward . . . promised in the Gospels, it would seem that our Lord finds our desires not too strong, but too weak. We are half-hearted creatures, fooling about with drink and sex and ambition when infinite joy is offered us, like an ignorant child who wants to go on making mud pies in a slum because he cannot imagine what is meant by the offer of a holiday at sea. We are far too easily pleased.[2]

So, we can be "far too easily pleased" or conversely far too easily displeased with our muddy lives. To appreciate our worth to God the Father, we need only look to the cross—to the sacrifice God made in sending his son, Jesus, to offer his life as a "ransom for many" and "while we were yet sinners." Our worth, in God's eyes, cannot be expressed quantitatively or even qualitatively, but relationally. We have worth because:

- God made us in his image.
- God in love sent Christ to die for sinners (you and me).
- God extended his mercy by refraining from giving us what we deserve.
- God extended his grace by giving us what we don't deserve.
- God has proclaimed us heirs—as sons and daughters—of his glorious kingdom.

God Don't Make Junk

Many of us have heard the above claims from childhood and believe them in our minds but have not embraced these truths in our hearts, still wondering how our worth will play out practically. Perhaps some of us feel like an old, battered musical instrument that hasn't been played in years—worn and out of tune from years of non-use. How can God use someone like me? Consider the following poem:

The Touch of the Master's Hand

'Twas battered and scarred, and the auctioneer
Thought it scarcely worth his while
To waste much time on the old violin,
But held it up with a smile.
"What am I bidden, good folks," he cried,
"Who'll start the bidding for me?
A dollar, a dollar. Then two! Only two?
Two dollars, and who'll make it three?
Three dollars, once; three dollars, twice;
Going for three . . ."

But no,
From the room, far back, a grey-haired man

Muddy People

Came forward and picked up the bow;
Then wiping the dust from the old violin,
And tightening the loosened strings,
He played a melody pure and sweet,
As a caroling angel sings.

The music ceased, and the auctioneer,
With a voice that was quiet and low,
Said: "What am I bid for the old violin?"
And he held it up with the bow.
"A thousand dollars, and who'll make it two?
Two thousand! And who'll make it three?
Three thousand, once; three thousand, twice,
And going and gone," said he.

The people cheered, but some of them cried,
"We do not quite understand.
What changed its worth?" Swift came the reply:
"The touch of the Master's hand."

And many a man with life out of tune,
And battered and scarred with sin,
Is auctioned cheap to the thoughtless crowd
Much like the old violin.

A "mess of pottage," a glass of wine,
A game—and he travels on.
He is "going" once, and "going" twice,
He's "going" and almost "gone."
But the Master comes, and the foolish crowd
Never can quite understand
The worth of a soul and the change that is wrought
By the touch of the Master's hand.[3]

"The Master's Hand" was written by Myra Brooks Welch, who came from a musical family and who played the organ as a young woman. However, she developed debilitating arthritis in later years, spending much of her time in a wheelchair and leaving her unable to perform music. Instead, she began writing poetry, using the eraser end of a pencil in each of her gnarled hands to painstakingly type out the words on a typewriter. Rather than become bitter about her disability, she embraced it, allowing it to stretch her abilities in other ways, all to God's glory.

When we consider our outer shells that God created, are we "comfortable in our own skin"? When we examine the reflection in the bathroom mirror, do we ever wonder if we measure up to society's standards of beauty or ruggedness? Do you look for ways to mask, alter, or even surgically change what your Creator already values? Do you ever feel like returning the "gift" for a refund or for an exchange for something better?

The way we respond to these questions says much about our view of God. If he truly created us in his image and we question our appearance or abilities, are we not judging God's wisdom to be inferior in some way? More possibly, are we doubting God's creative capacity to use us in any way he sees fit? Paul reminds us that "power is perfected in weakness" (2 Corinthians 12:9) and that we have this "treasure in earthen vessels, so that the surpassing greatness of the power will be of God and not from ourselves" (2 Corinthians 4:7).

Unfortunately, many of us consider ourselves to be "damaged goods." Perhaps we've given in to the Enemy's lies—to his denunciations—that we are not good enough in God's eyes. "If you resort to self-condemnation," says Derek Prince, "you are doing the devil's job for him in your own life. If you are a new creature in Christ, when you criticize yourself, you are criticizing God's handiwork. That is not your job. Don't do it!"[4]

On the other hand, maybe we allow our backgrounds—our family history, our addictions, our failed relationships—to define us. We may think, *God can't use someone like me given my checkered past. Surely there's someone else more worthy—more acceptable—than I am.* If that's you, then consider the following story:

> An elderly Chinese woman had two large pots hung on the ends of a pole that she carried across her neck. One of the pots had a crack in it, while the other pot was perfect and

Muddy People

always delivered a full portion of water. At the end of the long walks from the stream to the house, the cracked pot arrived only half full.

For a full two years this went on daily, with the woman bringing home only one and a half pots of water. Of course, the perfect pot was proud of its accomplishments. But the poor cracked pot was ashamed of its own imperfection, and it was miserable that it could do only half of what it had been made to do.

After two years of what it perceived to be bitter failure, it spoke to the woman one day by the stream. "I am ashamed of myself, because this crack in my side causes water to leak out all the way back to your house."

The old woman smiled. "Did you notice that there are flowers on your side of the path, but not on the other pot's side? That's because I have always known about your flaw, so I planted flower seeds on your side of the path, and every day while we walk back, you water them.

"For two years I have been able to pick these beautiful flowers to decorate the table. Without you being just the way you are, there would not be this beauty to grace the house."[5] (Author unknown)

Reflecting on this parable, what do you relate to more—the perfect vessel or the cracked pot? Most of us would undoubtedly compare ourselves to the imperfect container. And in all honesty, none of us passes muster in the flawlessness department. Yet God often chooses weaker, even cracked seemingly useless vessels to make his glory known. We only need look at the Apostles Paul and Peter, Moses, and even King David to understand that God ordains ordinary, fallible people to fulfill his purposes. And what of Jesus? Even though he lived a perfect, sinless existence on earth, his body—his earthen vessel—was broken on our behalf so that the Father's light could shine three days later through the risen Son!

So, do you qualify as a cracked pot, imperfect and unable to hold water but able to shine God's light and allow God's living water to flow through your "cracks"?

I know I do.

Cracked but Not Broken

So where do you fall on the spectrum between self-glory and self-deprecation? How do you react to God's creation of the unique "you"—tending to overemphasize your earthly attributes in vainglory fashion or downplaying your God-given talents, qualities, and gifts? Are you content to (à la C. S. Lewis) "play in the mud," or can you picture yourself from God's vantage point—a "living breathing priceless work of art"?*[6]

How does knowing that you have worth in God's eyes affect your thinking? Spend some time meditating on the fact that God made us in his image, loved us enough to send Christ to die for us, extended his grace and mercy, and declared us his sons and daughters—then offer a prayer of thanksgiving, asking God to help you grow more into Christ's image each day. Read Psalm 139:14 out loud to yourself as you gaze in a mirror.

In what areas of your life do you see God demonstrating his power through your weaknesses? Where is he continuing to mold and shape you? Allow God through his Holy Spirit to guide you into taking more risks and learning new ways to lean into him as you discover the person you were created to be. "God chooses to shine through imperfect, cracked pots," says Joyce Meyer. "People are blessed when our cracked pots let the light of Jesus shine through. Choose to be a glory-filled, cracked pot rather than an empty, pretty vessel."[7]

> As the clay yields to the potter, so the Christian must submit to the authority of God.... As the clay must be refined, so too must the Christian be refined before he can be shaped into a useful vessel by the Master Potter. (Bryant G. Wood)

Muddy People

*Consider listening to Steven Curtis Chapman's song, "Fingerprints of God," to give you a better perspective.

Chapter 2:
Nothing to Wear
(Fig Leaves Optional?)

> Adam and his wife were both naked, and they felt no shame. (Genesis 2:25)

> We are all born naked into this world, but each of us is fully clothed in potential. (Emmitt Smith)

Apparently, we were created *not* to wear clothes. Put another way, God did not *intend* for us to wear clothes. In a culture known usually for modesty, the thought of being *au naturel* beyond the privacy of our own homes probably makes most of us uncomfortable. Yet God's first children were oblivious to being sans clothes. As innocent and naïve as newborns, Adam and Eve were the first (only?) humans to bare all while bearing nothing (i.e., embarrassment). Theirs was a guiltless existence from the start, a carefree life that only required that they care for the land and the animals. God provided for their every need and granted them certain freedoms if only...

If only.

As cited in Genesis 2, God pretty much gave Adam free rein in the Garden of Eden. He could plant, cultivate, prune, harvest, and essentially eat from any tree or vegetation in the garden *if only* he did not eat from the tree of the knowledge of good and evil. And just to make sure Adam got the message, God added the following disclaimer:

> *Warning: Anyone eating from this tree of the knowledge of good and evil may experience the following side effects—uncommon awareness and insight into right and wrong leading to certain death.*

Huh. It seems sort of oxymoronic that ingesting a piece of fruit that could open your eyes to truth could also be your last meal. And notice that God made it abundantly clear that eating from this tree had definite consequences. He didn't say one could die or one might die but one will *surely* die. Make no mistake, Adam. There will be a corpse before the day is over if you eat from this tree! As stated in the Message, "The moment you eat from that tree, you're dead."

So what point was God trying to make? And why would he even allow the temptation to eat from the tree in the first place (when he knew the potential for disaster)? To answer that, we must look at the tree of knowledge metaphorically. Eating from the tree was definitely *verboten*—not because God said so or because the fruit was poisonous or because there were better trees to choose from. Rather, eating from *that* tree would lead to actually possessing the knowledge of good and evil and the ability to discern truth. While God had made humans in his image, he did not make them equal with him. To eat from the tree would have given man the capability to be on the same plane as the Creator—to become as God himself.

In many ways, we present-day people have taken part in our own version of the tree of knowledge. We attempt to control our own lives and destinies by our choices and decisions and by subconsciously yet blatantly shutting out God. We think we know best about what we want or need and where we need to invest our time, money, and resources (even whether a PC or a Mac will bring completion to our lives!). And in our digital age, we have succumbed to a rather popular but insidious notion. As post-moderns, we've perfected the art of browsing, texting, tweeting, blogging, and skyping. Information or knowledge has become the currency of the present age. He with the most blogs, the most "Likes," the most website hits, is the winner. Subsequently, the need for a Creator has become obsolete (or at least, something we can pull off of the shelf when we have the urge or necessity). Ah, if only God had a Facebook page or Twitter account.

Yes, a little knowledge is a dangerous thing (but with knowledge comes responsibility). Which brings us back to our main characters...

Genesis 3:7 reads that when Adam and Eve ate of the forbidden fruit, then "the eyes of both of them were opened and they realized they were naked." Notice that neither of them were immediately struck down by a lightning bolt, nor did they succumb to choking to death on the fruity morsel (thank goodness, since they didn't know about the Heimlich maneuver back then). No, but the physical death would eventually come. What was once immortal became mortal. Humans would not live physically forever as God intended. More importantly, the eating from the tree of knowledge ultimately led to a different kind of demise—the death of innocence. The full expression of free will allowed for the choice to love God and keep his commandments, as well as the choice to ignore God and disobey his directives. God was willing to take the chance to give humans the ability to love in return (aka true love) as opposed to programmed or forced love (which isn't love at all). But with that chance came also the opportunity to choose disobedience and ultimately, mortality.

Shamey, Shamey

> Man is the only animal that blushes. Or needs to. (Mark Twain)

The resulting "shame" from Adam and Eve's original sin of disobedience is woven into our consciences as a reminder when we fall short of God's laws and rules for living. When we try to re-label or reframe shame into something it is not, or attempt to qualify it as no longer relevant, we are assuming we know better than God what boundaries should be drawn and what counts as acceptable behavior or comprises our social mores. Whether we buy into the "Everybody's doing it" or the "If it feels good do it" mentality of the 60s and 70s, or the relativistic worldview of "What's right for me may not be right for you," we are abandoning those absolute truths that God established early on with, "Thou shalt not eat from that tree."

Over time, repeated sin comes to massage our guilt mechanism into interpreting our bad behavior in relative terms. We resort to a tendency to rationalize (or create *rational lies*, as Pastor Rick Warren has pointed out) and make excuses for sinful behavior. *Yes, I cheat a little on my taxes but not on my wife*, one may say. Or *At least I'm not a mass murderer or serial killer*, says another. But what it boils down to is that "we have forty million reasons for failure but not a single excuse" (in the words of Rudyard Kipling). In many ways, we're much like the king in the popular children's tale who failed to recognize his—well, let's read the story for ourselves:

The Emperor's New Clothes
(paraphrased from Hans Christian Andersen)

In this story, a vain emperor is known for his lavish taste in fine clothes. He is so obsessed with his wardrobe that he spends little time doing anything else. One day, two swindlers arrive at the castle, pretending to be tailors. They explain to the emperor that they can make him the finest clothing in the land—so fine, in fact, that it is made of a special material that becomes invisible only to those who are foolish or unfit for their office. The emperor hires the tricksters, who pretend to work feverishly all night to create the new set of clothes, but who actually create nothing. The emperor, not wanting to appear foolish, wears what is actually nothing in the royal procession. The crowd of townspeople, not wanting to appear foolish or unfit themselves, maintain the pretense of admiring the emperor's new but unseen clothes. It is only when an innocent child calls out, "But he has no clothes on!" that the people feel free to acknowledge what they see. The emperor, now realizing that he is truly wearing nothing, continues the charade by marching on with his head held high, too proud to admit he had been cheated.

Like the emperor in the story, you and I sometimes fail to recognize our own "nakedness" before God. We are blinded by our own pride while our sense of shame (a euphemism for nakedness) is either distorted or diminished. Much like our tendency to become desensitized over time to graphic displays of violence, language, or sex in the media, our souls too can become deadened to standards of morality and decency. As we allow the serpentine power of persuasion to entice us with words and promises of a better life, we become convinced that shame or even guilt may be overrated, outdated concepts. This might be best illustrated by the release of a film titled *Sex Tape*, which featured two popular actors. In the film, the two portray a husband and wife who decide to spice up their love life by creating a tape of their sexual activities. As is the case with many sex tapes, the supposedly private film mistakenly becomes public, in this case via the Cloud network. When interviewed about the filming of certain "awkward" scenes in the movie, the lead actor proclaimed that he and his co-actor (who aren't married in real life) "were really kind of spur-of-the-moment with it. What was really amazing about doing it with [her] is I think she and I come from a similar place when it comes to comedy. We don't have a tremendous sense of pride or shame."[1]

As I am writing this, there also seems to be a trend on reality TV in which nudity is part and parcel to the show's theme. One show titled *Naked and Afraid* follows the journeys of two strangers (one male, one female) as they traverse a remote wilderness location with only a few necessary survival items, their survival instinct, and the clothes on their own—wait, did I mention they are both naked?

Seemingly, the creators of the show felt that another "survival" show would do nothing for ratings or boost viewership unless there was something to grab a viewer's attention. "I know!" I can imagine one writer exclaiming. "Let's have them be naked." And so, for those who tune in to watch, we meet two complete strangers who are introduced for the first time *sans clothes*. After getting over the initial "awkwardness" (also known as "shame") of meeting a complete stranger *au naturel*, the couple proceeds to navigate the barren wilderness toward an agreed-upon site while confronting the elements. Obviously, to appease the FCC rules, the participants' private parts are carefully obscured (but not their derrieres). As one "contestant" stated later when interviewed about the nudity, "The naked factor goes away within an hour, once you realize what you have to do to survive."[2] Another participant said, "I was quite comfortable getting naked. It didn't bother me. Once we were out of our clothes, there was a comfort level achieved and I never looked back."[3] At the same time, she felt the urge to place her bag over her behind since that wasn't blurred out. "I was trying to maintain some sense of modesty," she said.

Other shows have followed suit, including *Dating Naked*, in which men and women meet and date at a secluded idyllic location, where the first "exposure" to each other is in the buff. The head of programming for the show reportedly approved the show her first day on the job, stating, "The idea of using nudity as a metaphor for allowing yourself to be truly exposed and truly yourself in the search for love felt really fresh and exciting."[4] Really.

It is interesting that the creators of these shows chose the titles that they did, rather than say, "Naked and Ashamed." In truth, "Shame runs deep in every sinner," writes Don Carson in his book *The God Who Is There: Finding Your Place in God's Story*, explaining why public nudity cannot lead to total transparency with others:

> The idea is that if you could be completely open and transparent in one part of your life, then sooner or later you could foster openness and transparency in every part of your life. So we begin with physical transparency—complete openness, nakedness—and maybe down the road we'll all become wonderfully open, candid, honest, caring, loving people. It never works. But that's the theory. The reason it never works is that we have so much to be ashamed of; there is so much we need to hide.[5]

Nothing to Wear

John Piper believes that God mercifully clothed Adam and Eve not so much as to cover their embarrassment but as a way of saying,

> You are not what you were, and you are not what you ought to be. The chasm between what you are and what you ought to be is huge. Covering yourself with clothing is a right response to this—not to conceal it, but to confess it. Henceforth, you shall wear clothing, not to conceal that you are not what you should be, but to confess that you are not what you should be. One practical implication of this is that public nudity today is not a return to innocence but rebellion against moral reality. God ordains clothes to witness to the glory we have lost, and it is added rebellion to throw them off.[6]

"Public nudity exposes a body," says Tony Reinke, "but more importantly it exposes a rebellious heart in denial. To be honest with God, honest with ourselves, and honest with others, we must keep our clothes on."[7] Moreover, nudity has been used in the Bible as a metaphor for helplessness and defenselessness, which is why as Reinke points out, "Public nudity is a fitting metaphor for God's judgment on sinners." What is more, Christ's *voluntary* sacrifice on the cross revealed his *involuntary* nakedness on our behalf so as to receive the full brunt of God's wrath against sin and evil and to remove our shame. Exposed and defenseless, Christ "stripped all the spiritual tyrants in the universe of their sham authority at the Cross and marched them naked through the streets" (Colossians 2:15, MSG). In the end, it's not that Christians are entertainment prudes but acknowledge public nudity in a way the world finds foolish or peculiar. For the Christian, "Christ's public nudity meant the utter defeat of Satan and victory for us."

Public nudity at its base is a form of moral and spiritual regression. "Taking your clothes off does not put you back into pre-Fall paradise" warns Piper. "It puts you into post-Fall shame."[8] As such, "public nudity is public hopelessness," says Reinke. "Public modesty, on the other hand, may seem like old cantankerousness in this culture, but it's designed by God to reflect a forward-looking and hope-filled longing."

Either way, our clothes (or lack of) say a lot about us, our identity, the hopes we believe, the lies we grasp, and how we think of our lives before God. "God, cover me!" is the Christian's true longing. We must escape this post-Fall nakedness. We must be covered by Christ. And we must keep the eschatological hope of resurrection burning in our souls, a longing so intense we find it now impossible to get comfortable in our own skin.[9]

Guilt by Association

So does the concept of guilt and shame still have relevance in today's society?* Or has it become a watered-down notion that finds its meaning within the prevailing cultural standards or worldview of relativism? First of all, we must distinguish between true guilt and false guilt. True guilt could be defined as a natural response to a moral breach of God's laws or commands. For example, the large majority of us would (hopefully) experience feelings of intense guilt were we to violate one of the Ten Commandments (e.g., stealing, cheating on a spouse, or murder). To not feel a twinge of regret in these situations would label you as either a sociopath (one who is incapable of feeling guilt or remorse) or at the very least, burdened with an underdeveloped or compromised conscience.

False guilt, on the other hand, deals with harboring regret for something we either did not do or should have done but with no moral absolute attached. One common example of false guilt deals with our need to please others—not that that is a bad thing (spoken in *Seinfeldese*). But when our happiness is dependent on making all people happy all the time, we set ourselves up to fail—miserably— and end up heaping coals of guilt upon our heads that have no toehold in truth. Likewise, many of us commit to serving God by overcommitting to doing *churchy* things. The busier we are, we reason, the more spiritual we must be (not to mention, if we don't do it, no one else will or at least not as well as we can). But busyness, as many of us have found out, is the devil's handiwork. It's the tempter's way of distracting us from what is true and right. It causes us to focus on doing rather than giving. A counselor once said that when it comes to busyness, the easiest cure for the accompanying false guilt and ironically the most affirming thing one can do is simply learn to say, "No."

The late author and psychiatrist John White reminds us in his book, *The Fight*, that Satan often uses false guilt as a weapon against believers. False guilt is "accuser-induced guilt," he states. The conscience is a helpful component of our psyches, but can it really be trusted? As White refers to an analogy by Donald Grey Barnhouse, the conscience can be likened to a sundial that works only with light from a proper source. It neither works in darkness, fog, or moonlight (nor even from a flashlight), but only by the sun's radiance. Similarly, one's conscience tends to function best when it has the "light of God's Word illuminated by God's Spirit, shining on it."[10]

Unfortunately, the simple act of becoming a Christian does not immediately tame our consciences to think or speak rightly. Wrong training and competing social voices serve to impede the conscience's proper functioning. In addition, while we may claim God's forgiveness, we still have difficulty forgetting past sins, preferring to cling to those memories. "If we don't allow the grace of God to saturate and sanctify our sinful memories," says Pastor Mark Batterson, "we continue to experience false guilt over confessed sin . . . [becoming] so fixated on past mistakes that we forfeit future opportunities."[11] To remedy the confusion between knowing the difference between Satan's accusations and the Spirit's true convictions, White suggests both long- and short-range plans. The lifelong process involves saturating ourselves in scripture— day by day, week by week, year by year—until the conscience is "reinstructed, reoriented by a progressive knowledge of God's Word." Much like a sailboat navigates by a corrected compass, so does the Christian conscience become more "finely and accurately tuned as practical experience in Scripture is gained under the

Spirit's tutelage."[12] Without that guidance from God's Word and the Holy Spirit, we become fair game to Satan's lies and dishonest indictments.

As for the short-term response, White points out that Satan's purpose in his accusations is to destroy fellowship with our Creator. The Spirit's motives, however, are to restore our communion with God. When we recognize true conviction from the Spirit and confess our sins, then the conviction will typically fade away while the "blossom of [restored] fellowship burst[s] out with new fragrance."[13] On the other hand, if we succumb to satanic accusations, we will not experience that aroma of restored fellowship. We may sense that our confession is inadequate in some way, leading us to continue searching and dredging for other, deeper levels of depravity that remain hidden because the Accuser—the Father of Lies—wants us to believe that Christ's redeeming blood is not sufficient.

Brennan Manning, in *The Ragamuffin Gospel*, states that we are "disdaining God's gift of grace" when we wallow in guilt and shame over sins of the past. And much of the cause for this unhealthy guilt is our preoccupation with self. When Christians fail, they fall into a vicious cycle of self-recrimination. "The language of unhealthy guilt is harsh," Manning asserts. "It is demanding, abusing, criticizing, rejecting, accusing, blaming, condemning, reproaching, and scolding."[14] In this state, it's almost as if we can't stand ourselves in God's presence. But it's because of God's presence, his compassion, and his forgiveness for our confessed wrongs that we can assume a healthy posture with our guilt, acknowledging our sins and feeling remorse, but then embracing God's offering of mercy and pardon. As Psalms 103:12 reminds us, "As far as the east is from the west, so far has he removed our transgressions from us." Claiming that promise, as well as Christ's redeeming blood, is a sure defense against the Accuser's evil deceit.

A Word on Shamelessness

Between the extremes of true guilt and false guilt, there is the whole notion of "no guilt." I'm not speaking of the grace-giving freedom that comes from knowing God and accepting Jesus as Lord and Savior ("Therefore, there is now no condemnation for those who are in Christ Jesus," Romans 8:1). Rather, it is a lack of guilt when guilt is due. It is lacking a natural sense of shame or remorse for a wrongdoing—for missing the mark (the true definition of sin).

As part of our human, sinful nature, we tend to find or invent ways to circumvent shame. We manage to take God's parameters for sin and redefine them in the context of our circumstances. This has its basis in the worldview of cultural and ethical relativism, but mostly has its roots in our own human pride and self-importance. The mantras of this perspective claim that "I know better than God what constitutes shame and guilt," "What may be shameful or sinful to you is acceptable to me (as long as it doesn't hurt anyone)," and "What may have been unacceptable in the past is no longer culturally relevant or is outdated in its notions." Obviously, there are still acts that most anyone would agree are reprehensible based on the Ten Commandments (murder being the most egregious), yet many of the remaining commandments have over time taken the form of the ten *suggestions* as humankind has gradually manipulated these once-given truths into more palatable versions. Over time, this takes the form of spiritual or moral paralysis—a numbing or deadening of the conscience toward absolute truth.

The Apostle Paul refers to this deadening of the conscience in his letter to the Ephesians, warning them of becoming complacent or buying into the prevailing culture of the day:

> So I tell you this, and insist on it in the Lord, that you must no longer live as the Gentiles do, in the futility of their thinking. They are darkened in their understanding and separated from the life of God because of the ignorance that is in them due to the *hardening of their hearts*. Having lost all sensitivity, they have given themselves over to sensuality

so as to indulge in every kind of impurity, and they are full of greed. (Ephesians 4:17–19, emphasis added)

Back to the Garden

When Adam and Eve were found naked and their sin exposed, Genesis 3 reports that they were ashamed. Until that time, the couple had no knowledge of shame, yet "the eyes of both of them were opened" to both good and evil upon eating the fruit. And while they knew only what was good prior to eating the fruit, the contrast of sin to their previous way of life must have been so hideous and repugnant that they cowered in shame, attempting to hide from God's judgmental eye. Or perhaps they realized that their "unwholeness" was in direct contrast to God's supreme and utterly pure holiness, much like Isaiah realized when in the presence of a holy God that he was a "man of unclean lips" (Isaiah 6:5).

Psychiatrist Curt Thompson suggests that the writer of Genesis intentionally chose shame over any of the other possible emotional states Adam and Eve could have experienced. (Why not naked and without fear or anger or sadness or disappointment or regret?) Rather,

> The writer wants us to pay attention to shame not just because it happens to show up later but because of its central role in all that ends in a curse. It is *the* emotional feature out of which all that we call sin emerges. As such, in the biblical narrative when we experience shame, we are not simply encountering one of an array of possible emotions; rather we are engaging evil in its most fundamental mode of operation. This is not unlike C. S. Lewis's sense of place of this emotion in our day-to-day lives: "I sometimes think that shame, mere awkward, senseless shame, does as much towards preventing good acts and straightforward happiness as any of our vices can do."[15]

Thompson further states that much of shame's stranglehold lies in its feature of hiding. "Whether it is the involution into the silence of our own minds or the literal turning away from someone with a downcast facial expression with eyes lowered, shame leads us to cloak ourselves with invisibility to prevent further intensification of the emotion."[16] As such, shame tends to be self-reinforcing. The very act of turning away from others causes shame to be intensified or reactivated. "Ironically," says Thompson, "the very act of alleviating our feelings of shame by turning away reinforces that shame we are attempting to avoid. We feel shame, and then feel shame for feeling shame. It begets itself."[17]

The best thing we can do to combat shame is to own it and to yield to vulnerability by opening ourselves to one another. But doing so can lead to a whole set of undesirable consequences. What if I'm rejected? What if no one likes the *real* me? Even worse, what if I end up being ostracized, isolated, or abandoned?

Returning to the Genesis story, God, being all-knowing, rather than confronting the first couple directly about their sin, posed the first recorded rhetorical question: *Where are you?* Now God knew very well where they were. It wasn't like their fig leaves camouflaged them from God's view. Or that this was some spiritual version of hide-and-seek and God was saying, "Okay, I give. Where are you two rapscallions?"

Rather, God begged the question for Adam and Eve's benefit. He needed to ask the question in order to draw them out. Left to their own devices, Mr. and Mrs. may have hidden themselves indefinitely because they had never before experienced this feeling of shame. How do you process something that you've never experienced firsthand? It was *not* a good feeling and one they could not shake. They were confused, troubled, and probably scared beyond belief.

But notice how they *did* respond. Like the proverbial child with his hand stuck in the cookie jar, Adam and Eve had no reasonable explanation at first. "I heard you," Adam replied, "and was afraid because I was naked. So I hid."

God proceeded with his peculiar line of questioning. "Who told you that you were naked?" And the follow-up: "Have you eaten from the tree that I commanded you not to eat from?"

Adam, realizing his window of opportunity, spoke first and cast the phrase that will forevermore drive a wedge into marital relationships. "The woman you put here with me," he said. "She gave me some fruit from the tree, and I ate it." Paraphrase: *That* woman (who shall remain nameless) that *you* gave me (yes, God—the one *you* gave me without consulting with me first) handed me some fruit (without telling me it was *that* fruit), so I ate it. And so, I rest my case."

God then turned to Eve to get her side of the story. "What is this you have done?" he asked.

The woman said, "The serpent deceived me, and I ate."

Isn't it interesting that God's virgin creatures had already become adept at passing the buck? Naturally, they wanted to avoid God's judgment at all costs, or at the very least, they didn't want to acknowledge that they had let him down by violating one of his commands. What they quickly realized was that nothing escapes God's all-knowing eye. "No creature is hidden from his sight," says the writer of Hebrews, "but all are naked and exposed to the eyes of him to whom we must give account" (Hebrews 4:13, ESV). Excusing one's behavior and poor choices only serves to obstruct God's natural order of confession and forgiveness. Yes, there must be consequences for sin. Much like breaking the speed limit or stealing from a store results in legal penalties, we must also incur God's judgment for breaking his laws.

But God, in his love and mercy and through his Son's sacrifice, offers that "second chance" to come clean and to return to fellowship with him. Marilyn Meberg, in her book *Tell Me Everything*, notes that while God did ultimately banish Adam and Eve from the Garden, along with their mortal destinies and hard labor, he also did a "most amazingly nurturing thing": "[He] made garments of skin for Adam and his wife and clothed them" (Genesis 3:21).[18] Having not known shame prior to their disobedience, the red-faced couple needed clothes. God did not allow them to wallow in their shame but pursued them, seeking their confession so that he could restore the fractured relationship and "clothe" them with his forgiveness.

Even today, he starts the conversation to redemption with "Where (or why) are you hiding?" He invites us to a frank and truthful appraisal of our sins. And with nowhere to hide, we must respond with naked honesty. As was stated earlier, God knows our motives, our thoughts, our desires, and our sinful natures. Yet he still asks the question to elicit our confession and ultimately return us to the path of experiencing his mercy, grace, and forgiveness. And, yes, restored relationship with the Creator of the universe.

Author Mark Buchanan ponders God's need to ask questions in his book *The Rest of God*:

> God, strictly speaking, has nothing to ask. But he asks anyhow. And this, I think, is why: nothing hooks us and pries us open quite like a question. You can talk all day at me, yet it obliges me nothing. I can listen or not, respond or not. But ask me one question, and I must answer or rupture our fellowship. God's inquisitiveness, his seeming curiosity, is a measure of his intimate nature. He desires relationship. He wants to talk *with us*, not just at us, or we at him.[19]

Nothing to Wear?

Ask yourself these questions: Do I have "nothing to wear" before a holy, omniscient God? Has his Spirit convicted me of any sin for "missing the mark" in some way? Have I tried in any way to become "as God" in thinking I know best what is right for me? What lies from Satan have I bought into? What forbidden fruits have I allowed myself to taste? Do I need to admit my "nakedness" and confess and repent of that sin? Is God calling out to me in my "hiding place"—calling me back to relationship with him, offering to "clothe" my shame with his grace, mercy, and love? Is there any "false guilt" that has served to sever my fellowship with God? Have I tried to redefine my shame in relative terms or refuse to acknowledge shame for what it is?

If we feel unworthy or unsuitable to acknowledge our faults and our missteps before God, or even if we have succumbed to a sense of false guilt, we have also been given the promise of Jesus' sacrifice and his cleansing power over sin and death to mediate on our behalf. Like a priest who has been granted authority to absolve us of all sin, Jesus serves as our Great High Priest (Hebrews 4:14–15). Even more, he was exposed to temptation as we are, yet he did not fall to sin. Who better to understand our predicament and to offer God's grace and mercy—free to all!

> "What then shall we wear?" Paul tells us in Romans 13:14: Wear Christ. "*Put on the Lord Jesus* Christ, and make no provision for the flesh, to gratify its desires." If you wear Christ, you will never hear any brave and wise soul cry out to you, "Shame on your nakedness." (John Piper)

*For purposes of this chapter, "guilt" and "shame" are used interchangeably, although many authors make a specific distinction between the two. Dr. Curt Thompson, among others, defines shame as a feeling that is deeply associated with a person's sense of self, apart from interactions with others (i.e., something I feel because I *am* bad). Guilt, on the other hand is the result of something I have done that negatively affects someone else (i.e., something I feel because I have *done* something bad).

Chapter 3:
Clothes Make the Man
(You Are What You Wear)

> Take each man's censure, but reserve thy judgment.
> Costly thy habit as thy purse can buy,
> But not express'd in fancy; rich, not gaudy;
> For the apparel oft proclaims the man.
> (William Shakespeare in *Hamlet*)

> Clothes make the man. Naked people have little or no influence on society. (Mark Twain)

As clothes became mainstay in human society, they took on greater significance, reflecting the various roles and status levels of the culture. Over time, clothes came to signify rank, class, role, and function. Those who claimed royalty wore clothes to reflect their authority. Priests donned garments to designate their role as God's ordained. Prisoners wore garb that denoted their status in society. And even 2,000 years before the birth of Christ, clothes distinguished between the haves and the have-nots—from kings to slaves and the common man in between.

Still today, the status assigned to clothing remains socially charged, often in the form of fodder relegated to the celebrity tabloids and gossip columns. What J.Lo or Jay-Z is wearing seems more newsworthy than the actual news. And why should we care? As parents (now of young adults), my wife and I often considered frugality and utility over show when dressing our young daughters. Certainly, we did not dress them shabbily or in such a manner that would bring ridicule, but neither did we go for the "popular" or prevailing name brands in our shopping habits. No, our children would be known for and take pride in what was "on the inside," not what others saw on the outside.

Apparently, this mindset caught on with various parent groups and even schools across the country. Today it is not uncommon for many public schools to adopt dress codes that seek to equalize the status of clothing among students. Having every student wear the same "uniform" eliminates the need to signify status by the type or brand of clothing that is worn. Someone who can't afford Tommy Hilfiger, J Crew, or Banana Republic won't be made to feel inferior or ostracized, as if they don't fit in or belong to a certain social or economic class. Even then, students find ways to express their individuality in unique ways, be it through displaying body adornments and tattoos, hiking up hemlines, or hiking down waistbands.

So do the types of clothes or apparel really matter in the end? According to research in the area of social psychology, it just may:

> What we wear affects how others perceive us. Women who wear more masculine clothes to an interview (such as a dress suit) are more likely to be hired. People dressed conservatively are perceived as self-controlled and reliable, while those wearing more daring clothing are viewed as more attractive and individualistic.[1]

Research, especially in the field of cognitive science known as embodied cognition, has revealed more compelling evidence. Embodied cognition, in essence, maintains that the mind directs the actions of the body, and that the body influences the mind—the idea that we think not only with our brains but also with our physical experiences. In a post by science writer Jordan Gaines Lewis, this could even include the clothes we are wearing.[2] Citing a study by Hajo Adam and Adam Galinsky of Northwestern University, Lewis describes an experiment in which the researchers assigned participants to separate conditions and experiments. In the first experiment, subjects were randomly assigned to a group in which they wore white lab coats or to a group wearing street clothes. The two groups then completed an incongruity task in which they were required to spot items that did not belong to a particular set (e.g., the word "red" written in green ink). Those subjects wearing the white lab coats made half as many errors as the other group.

In a second experiment, subjects were assigned to one of two conditions: one in which they believed they were wearing a doctor's lab coat and one in which they thought they were wearing a white painter's coat (actually identical to the doctor's coat). Initially, the two separate groups were assigned a task in which they were to closely examine two similar pictures, looking for minor differences between the two. The subjects who wore the *presumed* doctor's coats spotted more differences than the subjects wearing (what they thought were) painter's coats. Next, the two groups were directed to examine a doctor's lab coat displayed nearby. They then wrote essays expressing their opinions on the unique qualities of each coat. Again, after completing the picture comparison task, the subjects wearing the white lab coats experienced the greatest improvement in task performance. The conclusion: Simply looking at the item did not affect behavior. According to Galinsky, we must "see and feel the clothes on our body—*experience it* in every way—for it to influence our psyche."[3] The subjects in these experiments not only looked more professional, but subconsciously they *felt* more professional as well. In this case, clothes literally did make the man (or woman).

Dressing for Success

Obviously, as Christians, we cannot fall into the trap of thinking that our worth and acceptance are tied into the clothing we wear. Nor can we judge others for their choice of clothing (or lack of). However, our "spiritual" adornments matter greatly to God as they reflect his glory and our worth in his eyes. What happens when we take this concept seriously? Consider the following story:

> A short story written by French playwright Henri Duvernois (1875–1937) describes the manner in which changing one's outward appearances affects the way others treat him. Entitled "Clothes Makes the Man," the story tells how three robbers plan to rob a wealthy home on a busy street. Two of the gang would do the job while the third robber, a man named Tango, stood watch in a policeman's uniform. Anyone passing by would not suspect a problem since there would be a policeman on patrol.
>
> Now Tango was not all that smart, but from the very beginning the uniform began to change his outlook. It fit well. It made his hulking body look good. He liked the fact that he had a shiny whistle, just like a real policeman. And so he began to act like a policeman. He proudly gave a salute to a passing police lieutenant, helped an old woman across the street, and even decided to take a drunk who was disturbing the peace to jail.
>
> At this moment his two fellow robbers came running out of the house they were robbing to stop him. One robber said, "You blockhead. You'll ruin the whole job. What are you doing?" He then struck Tango across the face.
>
> Something snapped inside Tango. He remembered the lieutenant answering his salute. He remembered the gratitude and admiration of the old lady he helped across the street. Tango liked playing the role of policeman. And so as his companions looked on in horror, Tango stuffed the shiny whistle into his mouth and blew a salvo of blasts long enough to bring all the police in Paris. He yelled, "Crooks, robbers! I arrest you. I arrest you in the name of the law."[4]

Isn't it interesting how, simply by virtue of the clothes he wore, Tango the criminal transformed into Tango the law enforcer? In essence, he *became* the police officer—he took on the identity and persona of one who wears a law enforcer's uniform.

Similarly, we as Christians can become who we act to be. "We're not professional crooks," says Pastor Glen VanderKloot, "but we [are] sinners. [And] in God's eyes, there are no degrees of sin. A sin is a sin is a sin" (quoted in Daniels).[5] However, taking a lesson from Tango, we can start by "putting on" that which seems unnatural to us and allow God to change our attitudes into more Christ-like thoughts and actions. As the Apostle Paul wrote to the Colossians: "As God's chosen people, holy and dearly loved, clothe yourselves with compassion, kindness, humility, gentleness and patience" (Colossians 3:12, NIV).

In the movie *Dave*, the main character, a man named Dave Kovic, was chosen to impersonate the president of the United States after the chief executive suffered a stroke, leaving him in a coma. Dave, who bore a striking resemblance to the president, began playing the role of the president, convincing everyone around him. Although he wasn't the president, and did not hold those qualifications, Dave carried on the charade to the point that he *felt* presidential and it became almost natural for him.

In the same way, we as Christ followers can emulate Christ-like qualities and attributes by "wearing" the clothing of his virtues even if we don't feel particularly compassionate, kind, or patient. If we wait until we do feel as such, Satan will do his best to make sure we never feel like it. "Even though those attributes are not natural for us," adds VanderKloot, "we can put them on. We can clothe ourselves with Christ-like actions and attitudes. We can act in Christ-like ways even if we do not feel it. Attitude often follows action."[6]

C. S. Lewis once said that we are to "dress up as Christ," and though it may seem contrived, it is, in fact, what we are ordered to do. He writes, "But there is also a good kind [of pretending], where the pretense leads up to the real thing. When you are not feeling particularly friendly but know you ought to be, the best thing you can do, very often, is to put on a friendly manner and behave as if you were a nicer person than you actually are. And in a few minutes as we have all noticed, you will be feeling friendlier than you were. Very often the only way to get a quality in reality is to start behaving as if you had it already."[7]

Alcoholics Anonymous has been known to encourage its members to "fake it 'til you make it." Marriage counselors advise couples who have fallen out of love to act as if they are in love until they are in love once again. In the end, clothing ourselves with Christ's attributes often means that we *act* like Christ even before we *feel* Christ-like. On our road to recovery and transformation, action often precedes attitude. So taking Colossians 3:12 to heart,

> It does not matter if we feel compassionate. We can still act with compassion.
> It does not matter if we feel kind. We can still be kind to others.
> It does not matter if we feel humble. We can still be humble.
> It does not matter if we feel gentle. We can still be gentle.
> It does not matter if we feel patient. We can still be patient.

As Christians, our "spiritual clothing" should reflect "what's on the inside"—our standing as followers of Jesus. To "wear" what is popular in the world's eyes—to blend in with the crowd in our attitudes, our speech, and our actions—does not fly with scripture:

> Therefore, as God's chosen people, holy and dearly loved, *clothe yourselves with compassion, kindness, humility, gentleness and patience.* Bear with each other and forgive one another if any of you has a grievance against someone. Forgive as the Lord forgave you. And over all these virtues *put on love*, which binds them all together in perfect unity. (Colossians 3:12, emphasis added)

> Our beauty should *not* come from outward adornment, such as braided hair and the wearing of gold jewelry and fine clothes. Instead, it should be that of *your inner self*, the

unfading beauty of a *gentle and quiet spirit*, which is of *great worth in God's sight*. (1 Peter 3:3–4, emphasis added)

For all of you who were baptized into Christ have *clothed yourselves with Christ*. (Galatians 3:27, emphasis added)

In her book *Wearing God*, author Lauren Winner expands on the metaphor of being clothed with Christ—that "God clothes us with God's own self."[8] In a sense, God not only clothes or adorns us with his image—he also "fashions" us into the mold of Christ. Just as our choice of clothes shape our identity (doctor, clergy, weekend warrior), so should the wearing of Jesus form us into something we are naturally not. But besides shaping our identity, clothes also tend to communicate to others the identity we wish to portray. As in the experiment conducted by Adam and Galinsky (when choosing to don a doctor's lab coat declares to the world that we want to be taken seriously and perhaps deserving respect and esteem), putting on Jesus' attributes conveys an individual who wishes to be known as a sincere and genuine follower of Christ.

Winner notes that "this notion of communicative clothing—and the idea that, as with a garment, Christians might wordlessly speak something of Jesus—is appealing."[9] This is especially true for many of us who are more timid in sharing our faith or for whom words do not come easily—who prefer to adhere to St. Francis' encouragement to "always remember to preach the Gospel, and if necessary, use words." It is in the same vein as Christ's directive to "let your light shine before others, that they may see your good deeds and glorify your Father in heaven." If we are truly clothed with Christ's attributes, qualities, and nature, then our "light"—our attitudes, actions, and even our words—will point to the One who designs our Christ-like wardrobe, who fashions us to be in his image. "I like to imagine that occasionally people I encounter know from my vesture that my affections are Godward," says Winner. "What we are asking for, of course, is not clothing that is more articulate, but that our disposition—which is on display, often to a greater extent than we wish—would be more congruent with the Jesus whom we wear."[10]

Suiting Up for the Game

Most any sports team, be it professional or amateur, is known for its uniform. The design, the logo, and even the colors give a team its "brand." Sports uniforms symbolize not only the team but also the school, organization, or city from which the team hails. If I mention "Scarlet and Gray," you know I would be referring to the Ohio State Buckeyes. A red letter "A" with a halo encircling it stands for the Los Angeles Angels baseball team. A flaming basketball shooting through a hoop signifies the Miami Heat basketball team. And the logo of a smiling Quaker gentleman is obviously my high school mascot, Quaker Sam. (We were known as the mighty Quakers—not the fighting Quakers. That would be an oxymoron).

When you're wearing your team's uniform, you're playing for something bigger than yourself. There's no "I" in the word "team," so goes the expression. So whether you suit up for the Cincinnati Bengals, the Cincinnati Bearcats, or the Cincinnati Youth Soccer League, you wear that jersey for the pride of team Cincinnati, be it the city, the college, or your local community. Likewise, you cannot afford to reflect badly on your coach and teammates by poor play or sportsmanship or inappropriate behavior off the field.

Such was the case during Super Bowl XXIII between the San Francisco 49ers and the Cincinnati Bengals. The night before the game, Cincinnati suffered a major setback when Stanley Wilson, the Bengals' best fullback and third-leading rusher, was found high on cocaine in his hotel room. It ended up being Wilson's third violation of the league's drug policy, resulting in a lifetime ban from the NFL. Some later said that the muddy conditions of the playing field that day were well-suited for Wilson's running style. "I think he'd have had a big day rushing the ball," said Head Coach Sam Wyche when interviewed several years later, "but we'll never know."[11] Obviously, Wilson had selfishly let down his team and the town of Cincinnati that day, possibly impacting the outcome of the game—a Bengals' loss to the 49ers, 20–16.

By comparison, offensive tackle Anthony Munoz may be considered one of the best players to wear a Bengals' uniform. Now enshrined in the Pro Football Hall of Fame, Munoz played for 13 seasons in Cincinnati before later retiring as possibly the best offensive linesman in NFL history. But there's more to Anthony Munoz than his playing exploits. A strong man of faith in Christ, Munoz started the Anthony Munoz Foundation to impact the lives of local youth in the Cincinnati Tri-State area. When asked what lessons he took from playing professional football, he mentioned committing to the physical and mental discipline of the game, learning to be punctual, working together with teammates regardless of their cultural or socioeconomic background, and remaining coachable and teachable. As for integrating his faith with athletics, Munoz came to realize that worshiping God was not just about going to church on Sunday mornings. It was about giving God his glory in all aspects of the athlete's life, including on the field. "Since God gave me that gift," he said, "it was my goal to make every single play a worship performance."[12] Is it no wonder that Anthony Munoz has become one of Cincinnati's favorite sons—a man who has represented his team, his city, and his faith well.

Our spiritual apparel as Christians is always on plain view for others to see. Whether we realize it or not, others are taking notice as to whether our words and actions line up with our claim to be "clothed with Christ." Our "uniform" as Christ followers bears witness to God's grace, as well as to our faithfulness, convictions, and particular worldview. As we enter the "game" of life each day, we must always be mindful of who we represent and whose life we reflect and avoid conducting ourselves in any way that might tarnish his image.

Lightweight and Comfortable, Too

Being clothed with Jesus' attributes and qualities—his very essence—is something all believers undoubtedly aspire to, yet the process of "becoming" can seem daunting or even discouraging at times.

Fortunately, Jesus himself made a unique invitation to those who wished to follow him:

> Come to me, all you who are weary and burdened, and I will give you rest. *Take my yoke upon you* and learn from me, for I am gentle and humble in heart, and you will find rest for your souls. For my yoke is easy and my burden is light. (Matthew 11:28–30, emphasis added)

In biblical times, and even up through today in many third-world countries, a yoke was and is a way of linking two animals (usually oxen or sturdy horses) to plow and cultivate soil for farming. The yoke in its most primitive version often consisted of a crossbeam with two connected wooden loops through which the animal's heads were inserted. As such, they could work together as a team to perform the task of plowing or pulling.

Yokes obviously connote some type of submission (for animals, compliance to their master holding the reins of the yoke or harness). When Jesus referred to his yoke being easy, there remains an element of submission, for when we become Christians, we commit ourselves to his rule and authority. Yet Jesus is a gentle and humble master—not one who would lead us astray, but one from whom we can learn and who provides us with rest and refreshment.

Additionally, yokes can join animals of unequal strength and abilities. In those cases, the stronger, more experienced animal can guide the less capable partner to stay the course and to maintain a straight furrow in the soil. When Jesus told his listeners to take on his yoke, we can assume that "his yoke is easy and his burden is light" because he, in fact, is yoked with us—he on one side and we on the other. As we navigate life, Jesus is right there guiding, encouraging, and steering us in the right direction. When distractions and temptations attempt to interfere with our progress, our Master keeps us in step with him. For many of us, this may mean learning a new way of walking or a new rhythm or cadence. But before long, we become so in sync with Jesus' manner of leading that it seems as if we are no longer bearing a yoke at all. Naturally, we can choose not to be yoked with Christ, but seeing the alternatives, why would we not choose to do so?

Don We Now Our Gay Apparel

As God's adopted children, he has, in a sense, placed his signet ring on our finger and his purple robe around us, signifying our royal heirship in his kingdom. As such, we must exemplify our adoption and inheritance by donning apparel that coincides with the character and qualities of our older brother, Jesus. And the more we "put on" his attributes, the more like him we will become.

So what does your spiritual "adornment" say about your walk with Christ? Can others discern your status as a Christ follower? Or does your garb cause you to blend in with the culture around you—a Christian *incognito*, if you will? Reflecting on Paul's letter to the Colossians, have you dressed yourself with the virtues of compassion, kindness, humility, gentleness, and patience? Are the fruits of the Spirit—namely, love, joy, peace, forbearance, kindness, goodness, faithfulness, gentleness, and self-control—evident in your spiritual attire? If so, your dress—your presentation—should be peculiar within the culture around you.

As we seek after God and grow in our desire to become more Christ-like, we will find the Father gradually changing our wardrobe to reflect his glory. As we welcome each new day, we will find ourselves naturally choosing garb that models Jesus' character, qualities, and attributes. Rather than wearing clothing that draws attention to ourselves, our spiritual attire should direct others to the One who breathes life and purpose into those he calls his children. Rather than displaying outward beauty that fades, our beauty should be that of the inner self—the "unfading beauty of a gentle and quiet spirit, which is of great worth in God's sight" (1 Peter 3:4). And rather than clothing that puts self above others, we should clothe ourselves with humility toward one another (1 Peter 5:5).

CLOTHED with CHRIST

As baptized Christians, we are new people in the Lord; to be clothed in Christ isn't a metaphor just for justification, for Christ's righteousness covering our sins and giving us a new legal standing before God. Being clothed in Christ means being a new person, one "created in righteousness and true holiness."[13]

Chapter 4:
I Wouldn't Be Caught Dead in That
(Fashion Faux Pas: What Not to Wear)

> So Jacob said to his household and to all who were with him, "Get rid of the foreign gods you have with you, and purify yourselves and change your clothes." (Genesis 35:2)
>
> The angel said to those who were standing before him, "Take off his filthy clothes." Then he said to Joshua, "See, I have taken away your sin, and I will put fine garments on you." (Zechariah 3:4)

Prior to his death in 2008, popular fashion critic Richard Blackwell was known for his annual "Worst Dressed" list in which he publicly panned female celebrities who seemingly broke the barriers of tasteful apparel. No celebs appeared to be unscathed from Mr. Blackwell's yearly vitriol—from Martha Stewart to Cher to (gasp) even the Queen of England. While many of the rich and famous took offense at being named to the infamous list, some actually were thankful for the notoriety. The general public, however, looked forward less to the names but more to Blackwell's clever play on words in his critiques. On one occasion, he referred to a celeb's fashion style as "dull, dowdy, and devastatingly dreary."[1] To another, he made the sardonic comment, "She dances in the dark—and dresses there, too."[2] Still another: "[She] packs all the glamour of an old, worn-out sneaker."[3]

Hyperbole aside, Blackwell claimed his innocence of character assassinations. In a statement made in 1998, the critic commented that he was simply offering his satirical view of the fashion world. "I merely said out loud what others were whispering.... It's not my intention to hurt the feelings of these people. It's to put down the clothing they're wearing."[4]

As it turns out, Richard Blackwell was not the first critic of unsightly attire. The Old Testament speaks of many Mosaic restrictions emphasizing God's desire for holiness and purity in his people. Deuteronomy 22:5, for example, refers to gender distinctions in that women should not wear men's clothing and vice versa, which was considered detestable in God's eyes. Deuteronomy 22:11 describes the restriction of combining certain fabrics, in this case, wool and linen. This may seem to be an irrational constraint on God's part, but some theologians theorize that the pagans of the day may have worn clothing of mixed fibers. This law may have been simply to set apart God's people from the neighboring heathens.

In Genesis 35, Jacob is told by God to go to Bethel and to build an altar—a symbol of a new beginning and of God bringing Jacob full circle from his brotherly deception of his twin Esau to Esau's ultimate show of compassion and forgiveness of Jacob. To further signify the act of restoration, Jacob tells his household to rid themselves of any false gods and to further "clean house" by changing their clothes. The act of putting on new, clean garments was to be an outward sign of an inward purifying of the heart.

Further evidence of God's desire to "make us over" can be found in Zechariah 3, when the prophet speaks of a vision in which the high priest Joshua stands before God representing the people of Israel. Symbolic of the Israelite's iniquities, Joshua appears in filthy, sin-stained clothes. God, in his desire to restore and purify his people, orders Joshua be fit with fine garments.

Clean clothes, then, were symbolic of the transformation God desired in his people. "I am the Lord your God; consecrate yourselves and be holy, because I am holy," God declares in the book of Leviticus. For his chosen people, the Israelites, holiness was achieved through both ritualistic purification and obedience to God's commandments. Not only were their lives supposed to reflect "holiness unto the Lord," but their outward appearance (including their clothing) also needed to pass the purity test.

Off With the Old, In With the New (Your Slip Is Showing)

What Not to Wear was a popular reality television series in which individuals were nominated by family and friends for fashion makeovers. Over a period of two weeks, the nominees were secretly videotaped going about their public lives in attire that was deemed deplorable by most fashion experts. The show's hosts then confronted the individuals with the evidence of their fashion faux pas, mercilessly casting out their outdated wardrobes in front of them, and providing professional consultations regarding clothing that would complement their body types, ages, and lifestyles. While many of the nominees on the show were initially offended by the notion that their wardrobes needed tweaking, by the end of the show most had embraced their new-found sense of identity, simply by making some much-needed changes in their closets.

In the same sense, God calls his children to revamp their wardrobes consistent with their identity as righteous heirs. Paul, in his letter to the Ephesians, stressed this point in this way:

> You were taught, with regard to your former way of life, to *put off your old self*, which is being corrupted by its deceitful desires; to be made new in the attitude of your minds; and to *put on the new self*, created to be like God in true righteousness and holiness. Therefore each of you must *put off* falsehood and speak truthfully to your neighbor, for we are all members of one body. (Ephesians 4:22–25, emphasis added)

CLOTHED with CHRIST

In this passage, Paul referred to the "clothes" of our character—our inward nature. When telling the church in Ephesus to "put off" their old selves, he was speaking of their earthly natures that were corrupted or "soiled" by "deceitful" or misguided desires of the heart. Paul was not speaking as some finger-wagging saint; he spoke from personal experience, having played an active role in persecuting Christians before his Damascus transformation. If anyone knew what it meant to "put off" the old self and "put on" the new, it was Paul. His miraculous makeover from schoolyard bully to peacemaker and apostle gave him the street cred to be able to say with conviction, "Ya'll need to get out of those filthy rags and start dressing like God's people!"

In his letter to the Colossians, Paul was even more direct and to the point:

> Put to death, therefore, whatever belongs to your earthly nature: sexual immorality, impurity, lust, evil desires and greed, which is idolatry. Because of these, the wrath of God is coming. You used to walk in these ways, in the life you once lived. But now you must also rid yourselves of all such things as these: anger, rage, malice, slander, and filthy language from your lips. Do not lie to each other, since you have *taken off your old self* with its practices and have *put on the new self*, which is being renewed in knowledge in the image of its Creator.... (Colossians 3:5–10, emphasis added)

Again, Paul referred to taking off the old self and putting on the new, likened to items of clothing. The old self (as noted in Ephesians 4) represents our old nature—that which is corruptible, fraudulent, and temporary. Moreover, it is known by the adornments it possesses—unrestrained anger, hatred, insulting and filthy language, and lying. Paul stated that one who claims faith in Christ is not to display these types of behaviors, no more than you would go out in public in clothing that was tattered, mismatched, or indecent. Like clothing that has outlived its usefulness and become essentially "rags," we are to take them off or discard them to the refuse pile, no longer to be worn again. In place of these cast-off remnants, we are to put on new "clothing" that conveys God's righteous and holy character, embellished with the accoutrements of compassion, kindness, humility, gentleness, and patience, with love being the final accessory to complete the ensemble. Moreover, we are to be filled inwardly and clothed outwardly with the power of the Holy Spirit (Luke 24:49), bearing the fruit of "love, joy, peace, forbearance, kindness, goodness, faithfulness, gentleness, and self-control" (Galatians 5:22–23). Now that's dressing for success!

Neither Self-Righteous nor Fashionable

Of course, Paul knew full well the war that raged within men's souls—between wanting to do right and our base urge to sin:

> So I find it to be a law that when I want to do right, evil lies close at hand. For I delight in the law of God, in my inner being, but I see in my members another law waging war against the law of my mind and making me captive to the law of sin that dwells in my members. Wretched man that I am! Who will deliver me from this body of death? (Romans 7:21–24, ESV)

Some Bible scholars relate Paul's use of the phrase "body of death" to the alleged Roman practice of binding the corpses of murder victims to the backs of the murderers as a form of torture or punishment. The guilty parties were required to literally carry around "dead weight" to remind them night and day of their crime.[5] This was unspeakably cruel and even barbaric by today's standards of criminal justice but effective, to be sure. But the allegory cannot be ignored: Before we can put on what is new, we must get rid of the excess baggage—the "dead man"—that we carry around on our backs.

If we are serious about spiritual transformation, then we must take seriously Paul's clear admonition to both "put [take] off" and to "put on." We cannot continue wearing outdated or unacceptable clothing while also donning new apparel. They are incompatible. Anger cannot coexist with love, insults do not complement compliments, and lies have no defense in light of the truth. In his letter to the Colossians (3:5–10), Paul is even more insistent in stating we are to "put to death" whatever belongs to our earthly natures. The Message bible translation states it more plainly: it means "killing off everything connected with that way of death . . . [that way of] doing whatever you feel like whenever you feel like it, and grabbing whatever attracts your fancy." In our former lives, Paul continues, we didn't know better. "But you know better now," he says, "so make sure it's all gone for good."

In his book *Discipline of Grace*, Jerry Bridges likens Paul's twofold approach of putting off/putting on to the two blades of a pair of scissors. "A single scissors blade is useless as far as doing the job for which it was designed. The two blades must work in conjunction with each other to be effective."[6] In a similar vein, we must intentionally put off the traits of our old former selves and put on the qualities indicative of our new glorious selves. It would be ineffective to our spiritual transformation to do one and not the other.*

What happens when we attempt to focus on one or the other? Believers who spend their lives putting off sinful practices and avoiding "thou shall nots" in the absence of putting on godly qualities end up becoming hard and brittle Christians, if not downright self-righteous. Other Christians may glory in cultivating positive traits such as love, compassion, and kindness but become careless in or lose sight of well-defined moral and ethical boundaries grounded in God's absolute truth, law, and righteousness. Jesus offered a similar caution in the Gospel of Mark:

> No one sews a patch of unshrunk cloth on an old garment. Otherwise, the new piece will pull away from the old, making the tear worse. And no one pours new wine into old wineskins. Otherwise, the wine will burst the skins, and both the wine and the wineskins will be ruined. No, they pour new wine into new wineskins. (Mark 2:21–22)

I Wouldn't Be Caught Dead in That

With these words, Jesus was proclaiming that God's Kingdom was not only at hand—it had arrived. It meant a new way of doing things and of thinking and of living. Gone was old, dyed-in-the-wool legalism and following rules. Instead, a new song was being sung, a hymn of God's mercy and grace and salvation. While God's wrath and judgment still remained resolute, it was being held in reserve until the right moment. Until then, God's people were to avoid mixing the new with the old. "No one cuts up a fine silk scarf to patch old work clothes; you want fabrics that match. And you don't put your wine in cracked bottles" (Mark 2:21–22, MSG).

Indentured or Free?

A review of early American history tells of the role that indentured servants played in our country's development. In exchange for a new life in America, poor and desperate immigrants from Europe pledged to work for colonial landowners for a specified number of years. At the end of their commitment, they were often given "freedom dues"—sometimes money or land to start them off in their new, emancipated lives, but most often a new set of clothes symbolizing their well-earned change in status. In the same manner, our spiritual "clothing" must reflect our new-found freedom in Christ and not our former selves who were bound to a different earthly master.

Perhaps it's human nature to want to stick with our old clothes because they're more comfortable, while new clothes don't always feel right when we first start wearing them. However, Jesus is quite clear in his invitation to join God's kingdom on earth: You must be born again (John 3:3). To be born again means not just a spiritual rebirth but also a fresh start. It means looking in the rearview mirror at those things that defined us before we declared our faith in Christ. It means "sinking the ships" that tempt us to return to what is comfortable or familiar and to face an unseen but known future that promises eternal security and adoption as God's children. In light of those promises, however, and in the meantime, we must dress the part.

CLOTHED with CHRIST

What's in Your Closet?

Looking through your "closet," what articles of "clothing" do you need to discard? What apparel have you been wearing that no longer fit the bill in keeping with your identity as a Christ follower? Do you harbor hostility or grudges toward anyone? Remove them and replace them with love. Do you engage in gossip, insults, or inappropriate language? Toss them out and "put on" language that is uplifting and pleasing, which builds up rather than tears down. Do you use lies to cover up your inadequacies and sins, or do you shade the truth to give a false impression to others? Shed these outdated coverings and dress yourself with truth, honesty, and righteous thoughts. Finally, is anger, rage, or an uncontrolled temper wreaking havoc in your relationships, causing others to avoid you or cower in your presence? Consider replacing your wardrobe with gentleness, humility, and patience.

> Being clothed in Christ is more than just a legal standing with God. Christians are united with Christ; they are surrendered to Him; and through Him they are being renewed, rejuvenated, and restored. Christians who refuse to change their old ways, their old habits, and their old lifestyle need to look in the mirror at what they are really clothed in.[8]
>
> He is ill clothed, who is bare of virtue. (Benjamin Franklin)

*This is consistent with research on habits. In his book *The Power of Habit*, Charles Duhigg explains that to change or replace one habit with another, we must insert a new competing response or routine into our habit "loops." Habit loops consist of a cue (something that triggers a response), which in turn becomes a routine that leads to a certain reward for responding to the cue.[7] So, within the realm of spiritual transformation, if we wish to "put off" the habit of anger or bitterness in response to a cue (e.g., getting cut off in traffic), we need to replace the response (e.g., calling the other driver names)

I Wouldn't Be Caught Dead in That

with a different routine (e.g., saying instead, "God bless you"). While the initial response of calling the other drive names may offer the reward of feeling better for having gotten it off our chest, blessing the other driver instead can also lead to a rewarding feeling or emotional release (but in the form of a blessing rather than a curse).

Chapter 5:
A Wolf in Sheep's Clothing
(God Sees the Deception)

>All that glisters is not gold—
>Often have you heard that told.
>Many a man his life hath sold
>But my outside to behold.
>Gilded tombs do worms enfold.
>Had you been as wise as bold,
>Young in limbs, in judgment old,
>Your answer had not been inscrolled.
>Fare you well. Your suit is cold.
>(William Shakespeare from *The Merchant of Venice*)

The expression "a wolf in sheep's clothing" has been with us for centuries, perhaps most attributed to a story told by Aesop of fable fame. The best known version of this cautionary tale comes from an 1867 translation by George Fyler Townsend, which presents the fable in this manner:

>Once upon a time a Wolf resolved to disguise his appearance in order to secure food more easily. Encased in the skin of a sheep, he pastured with the flock, deceiving the shepherd by his costume. In the evening he was shut up by the shepherd in the fold; the gate was closed, and

the entrance made thoroughly secure. But the shepherd, returning to the fold during the night to obtain meat for the next day, mistakenly caught up the Wolf instead of a sheep, and killed him instantly.[1]

Over time, society has come to use the phrase to refer to someone who hides malicious intent under the guise of kindliness or innocence. Or put more simply, someone who pretends to be something or someone he is not.

Jesus, perhaps alluding to Aesop's well-known tale, also warned against wolves in sheep's clothing:

> Beware of false prophets, who come to you in sheep's clothing but inwardly are ravenous wolves. By their fruit you will recognize them. (Matthew 7:15)

The Apostle Paul, too, in addressing believers in Corinth and in Ephesus, cautioned against those who pretended to be leaders of the church:

> For if someone comes to you and preaches a Jesus other than the Jesus we preached, or if you receive a different spirit from the Spirit you received, or a different gospel from the one you accepted, you put up with it easily enough.... For such men are false apostles, deceitful workmen, disguising themselves as apostles of Christ. And no wonder, for even Satan disguises himself as an angel of light. So it is no surprise if his servants, also, disguise themselves as servants of righteousness. Their end will correspond to their deeds. (2 Corinthians 11:4, 13–15)

> Pay careful attention to yourselves and to all the flock, in which the Holy Spirit has made you overseers, to care for the church of God, which he obtained with his own blood. I know that after my departure fierce wolves will come in among you, not sparing the flock; and from among your own selves will arise men speaking twisted things, to draw away the disciples after them. (Acts 20:28–30)

A Wolf in Sheep's Clothing

While Jesus was referring to false prophets and Paul to deceitful and greedy leaders, they could have just as well been referring to those in the "flock" who claimed to be Christ-followers but whose actions and priorities were not consistent with Christian teachings. Today we sometimes refer to these folks as "false" or "carnal" Christians—individuals who may have experienced a true conversion experience but have since fallen away or who choose to live merely as "Sunday morning" Christians (1 hour/1 day vs. 24/7). While good people in the sense of having decent morals, following the rules of society, and basically giving "God his due" when it is appropriate, they give the appearance of being Christians but only in right amounts. After all, no one wants to be labeled as "radical" or "too righteous" when it comes to religion. The funny thing, though, is that Jesus talked about this in the same breath as his wolf reference:

> "Not everyone who says to me, 'Lord, Lord,' will enter the kingdom of heaven, but only the one who does the will of my Father who is in heaven. Many will say to me on that day, 'Lord, Lord, did we not prophesy in your name and in your name drive out demons and in your name perform many miracles?' Then I will tell them plainly, 'I never knew you. Away from me, you evildoers!'" (Matthew 7:21–23)

Later in John's book of Revelation, Christ offers a more blunt description of casual Christians:

> I know your deeds, that you are neither cold nor hot. I wish you were either one or the other! So, because you are lukewarm—neither hot nor cold—I am about to spit you out of my mouth. (Revelation 3:15–16)

Obviously, there are the extremes of sheep's clothing that come to mind—clergy, teachers, or other adults who are held in the public's trust but who use their positions for self-serving purposes to prey on vulnerable young people. However, there are probably many more "garden variety" types of sheep-aka-wolves in our midst than we care to admit (present company included). I imagine that many of us look in our "closets" each day to find that one woolly outfit that will disguise our true selves to the outside world. Perhaps to hide our pornography addiction, we present to our peers as morally upright and supportive of women in the workplace. To disguise our alcohol or substance abuse, we contrive stories and lies to hide the truth from family and friends. Or maybe it's even more subtle by using our Christian faith as a pretense to massage our egos or to build pride in ourselves. Masquerading as Christians, however, should not be taken lightly.

"Impostors in the Spirit always prefer appearances to reality," claims Brennan Manning. "Rationalization begins with a look in the mirror. We don't like the sight of ourselves as we really are, so we try cosmetics, makeup, the right light, and the proper accessories to develop an acceptable image of ourselves. We rely on the stylish disguise that has made us look good or at least look away from our true self. Self-deception mortgages our sinfulness and prevents us from seeing ourselves as we really are—ragamuffins."[2]

Author and pastor Mark Buchanan suggests that rather than appearing as wolves in sheep's clothing, many Christians act more like sheep in sheep dog's clothing, "concealing our docility and waywardness beneath a disguise of master-pleasing eagerness." Appearing better than we really are, he says, we tend to employ a ruse of over-performance that "hides a mother lode of apathy—[a] display of virtue that is just that, a display." Over time, Buchanan points out, the deception runs its course as it becomes evident that it's "exhausting to keep building the edifice of good behavior on a foundation of sticks."[3]

One Foot in the Grave

Jesus used another expression, perhaps even more uncomplimentary than sheep shirts:

> Woe to you, teachers of the law and Pharisees, you hypocrites! You are like whitewashed tombs, which look beautiful on the outside but on the inside are full of the bones of the dead and everything unclean. In the same way,

on the outside you appear to people as righteous but on the inside you are full of hypocrisy and wickedness. (Matthew 23:27–28)

The Message translation is even more descriptive:

> You're hopeless, you religion scholars and Pharisees! Frauds! You're like manicured grave plots, grass clipped and the flowers bright, but six feet down it's all rotting bones and worm-eaten flesh. People look at you and think you're saints, but beneath the skin you're total frauds. (MSG)

Sounds like a description from the show *The Walking Dead*. But in these passages, Jesus was clearly calling out the teachers of the law for their obsession with outward rituals and "thou shalt nots." In present-day language, we refer to this emphasis on rules and conduct at the expense of grace, mercy, and love as *legalism*. The Pharisees of Jesus' day were most guilty of this in that they obsessed on the letter of the law rather than the spirit. Haughty and proud, this group of sanctimonious scoffers relied on nitpicking their way into God's kingdom but failed to see God's kingdom right in front of their brown-tinged noses. Jesus, of course, saw through their heightened sense of superiority and called them out:

> "Woe to you, teachers of the law and Pharisees, you hypocrites! You give a tenth of your spices—mint, dill and cumin. But you have neglected the more important matters of the law—justice, mercy and faithfulness. You should have practiced the latter, without neglecting the former. You blind guides! You strain out a gnat but swallow a camel." (Matthew 23:23–24)

Ahh, nothing like a good dose of Jewish sarcasm and hyperbole to paint a visual image that is nothing short of righteous comeuppance. Had Jesus been a stand-up comedian, the story might have gone like this:

> Did you hear about the Pharisee who found a fly in his soup? "Waiter," he said, "what's this fly doing in my soup?"

"I'm not certain," said the waiter, "but it seems to be doing the backstroke around that camel." *(Drum roll with cymbal crash)*

Jesus' use of the word "hypocrites" in his admonition to the Jewish leaders and Pharisees originates from the Greek *hypokrites*, meaning "actor." In ancient classical theater, Greek actors who played several parts often wore a different mask to portray each role. Similarly, as Christians, we often hide behind masks of our own making and get caught up in what others see on the outside. But what others see isn't always what's on the inside. That's what Jesus was railing against with the teachers of the law whose teaching didn't reflect who they really were in their hearts.

Fans or Followers?

Kyle Idleman, in his book *Not a Fan*, notes that many individuals claim to be followers of Jesus but in actuality are just fans. One of his acid test questions for diagnosing fandom is to ask yourself, *Am I more focused on the outside than the inside?* If you're choosing rules over relationship, then you're probably bound by legalism. If you choose laws over love, then you're more concerned with the external than the internal. If you're focused on the "do's" of religion, then you're weighed down by fear and guilt. But if you claim the "done" of God's unmerited gift, you're motivated by grace.

> These religious types were the fans that Jesus seems to have the most trouble with. Fans who will walk into a restaurant and bow their heads to pray before a meal just in case someone is watching. Fans who won't go to R-rated movies at the theater, but have a number of them saved on their DVR at home. Fans who may feed the hungry and help the needy, and then they make sure they work it into every conversation for the next two weeks. Fans who make sure people see them put in their offering at church, but they haven't considered reaching out to their neighbor who lost a job and can't pay the bills. Fans who like seeing other people

A Wolf in Sheep's Clothing

fail because in their minds it makes them look better. Fans whose primary concern in raising their children is what other people think. Fans who are reading this and assuming I'm describing someone else. Fans who have worn the mask for so long they have fooled even themselves.[4]

Fortunately, when we have given our hearts to Jesus, he is tender and encouraging, even if we don't have it all together on the inside. "Jesus doesn't expect followers to be perfect, but he does call them to be authentic," says Idleman. "Someone who isn't pretending on the outside to have it all together."[5] But being human, we sometimes choose following rules over our relationship with our heavenly Father. However, when that relationship on the inside is true and right, external actions will follow. Conversely, when we make rules more important than loving people—when rules take precedent over relationships—then we're acting more like fans of than followers of Jesus. When following rules becomes our *modus operandi*, then guilt often becomes the primary motivating factor. When we focus on doing enough or checking off spiritual "to-do" lists to earn God's favor, we end up exhausted and guilt-ridden because we can never keep up the pace of "keeping up." Are we followers then of Christ or followers of religion?

Idleman shares one story of a father who spoke of his daughter who was raised in a Christian home and attended church faithfully, only to leave the faith in her young adult years. With tears in his eyes, the father captured the essence of his daughter's decision: *"We raised her in Church, but we didn't raise her in Christ."* Translation: When you're raised to look right on the outside but neglect the inside, when you're taught to keep the rules but ignore relationship, when you're made to feel guilty for the wrong things you did, then you miss out on God's amazing grace. You've been taught to be a fan of Jesus instead of a follower.[6]

Jesus obviously made a point of exposing the Pharisees' hang-ups regarding rules with vivid denunciations that left no doubts about his intentions or his blameless nature. This is the same Jesus who earlier had challenged the crowd of angry teachers of the law who wanted to stone a woman guilty of adultery. "Let he who is without sin cast the first stone," Jesus had replied. Fast forward to his comments about white-washed tombs and swallowing camels, Jesus could not have made these acrid accusations unless he himself was without sin. His pure and holy nature gave him the absolute right to denounce the Pharisees in the manner he did. His love and compassion for the woman prevented him from stoning her himself, which he was entirely in his right to do under Mosaic Law.

Even today, Jesus is ready and willing to forgive our sins, just like the woman who had committed adultery. Yet, he also has little patience—in fact, *no tolerance*—for sheep-clothed Christians.

Apple Polishers or Fruit Bearers?

Jesus also made it clear that many would try to follow him but fall short. In the parable of the sower, he distinguishes between those who hear his words and do them and those who do not:

> "A farmer went out to sow his seed. As he was scattering the seed, some fell along the path, and the birds came and ate it up. Some fell on rocky places, where it did not have much soil. It sprang up quickly, because the soil was shallow. But when the sun came up, the plants were scorched, and they withered because they had no root. Other seed fell among thorns, which grew up and choked the plants. Still other seed fell on good soil, where it produced a crop—a hundred, sixty or thirty times what was sown. Whoever has ears, let them hear." (Matthew 13:3-9)

Naturally, Jesus' followers pondered his words, trying to make sense of the stories he often told that had apparent deeper meaning. The disciples (or *duh*-ciples as one bible scholar puts it)[7] asked Jesus, "Oy vay, Rabbi! There you go again with the stories! Why do you tell such tales?" Jesus then provided his own commentary:

> "Listen then to what the parable of the sower means: When anyone hears the message about the kingdom and does not

A Wolf in Sheep's Clothing

understand it, the evil one comes and snatches away what was sown in their heart. This is the seed sown along the path. The seed falling on rocky ground refers to someone who hears the word and at once receives it with joy. But since they have no root, they last only a short time. When trouble or persecution comes because of the word, they quickly fall away. The seed falling among the thorns refers to someone who hears the word, but the worries of this life and the deceitfulness of wealth choke the word, making it unfruitful. But the seed falling on good soil refers to someone who hears the word and understands it. This is the one who produces a crop, yielding a hundred, sixty or thirty times what was sown." (Matthew 3:18-23)

Jesus knew who his real followers were—the ones who bore fruit. They were doers and not hearers only. Earlier, he had warned his followers of the consequences of bearing or not bearing fruit:

> By their fruit you will recognize them. Do people pick grapes from thornbushes, or figs from thistles? Likewise, every good tree bears good fruit, but a bad tree bears bad fruit. A good tree cannot bear bad fruit, and a bad tree cannot bear good fruit. Every tree that does not bear good fruit is cut down and thrown into the fire. Thus, by their fruit you will recognize them. (Matthew 7:16-20)

Obviously, the act of bearing fruit assumes doing so with pure and godly motive. If we focus on external appearances and looking good, our acts are rooted in hypocrisy cloaked as honorable deeds. Brennan Manning again:

> The noonday devil of the Christian life is the temptation to lose the inner self while preserving the shell of edifying behavior. Suddenly I discover that I am ministering to AIDS victims to enhance my resume. I find I renounced ice cream for Lent to lose five excess pounds. I drop hints about the absolute priority of meditation and contemplation to create the impression that I am a man of prayer. At some

unremembered moment I have lost the connection between internal purity of heart and external works of piety. In the most humiliating sense of the word, I have become a legalist. I have fallen victim to what T.S. Eliot calls the greatest sin: to do the right thing for the wrong reason.[8]

Theologian J. I. Packer put it this way (additions in italics added):

> The mark of the false prophets [*Christians*] is self-serving unfaithfulness to God and His truth.... There are teachers [*Christians*] in the church today who never speak of [*believe in*] repentance, self-denial, the call to be relatively poor for the Lord's sake, or any other demanding aspect of discipleship. Naturally they are popular and approved, but for all that, they are false prophets [*Christians*]. We will know such people by their fruits.[9]

While we may be able to deceive others, our ruse does not escape the knowing eyes of Jesus. To think we can avoid detection is to deny that Jesus is who he said he was or that his words in John 10 don't ring true. But how does he know who belongs to him and who doesn't? Perhaps a contemporary tale can shed some light:

The Shepherd's Voice

> A man in Australia was arrested and charged with stealing a sheep. But he claimed emphatically that it was one of his own that had been missing for many days. When the case went to court, the judge was puzzled, not knowing how to decide the matter. At last he asked that the sheep be brought into the courtroom. Then he ordered the plaintiff to step outside and call the animal. The sheep made no response except to raise its head and look frightened. The judge then instructed the defendant to go to the courtyard and call the sheep. When the accused man began to make his distinctive call, the sheep bounded toward the door. It was obvious that he recognized the familiar voice of his master. "His sheep know him," said the judge. "Case dismissed!" Those who

A Wolf in Sheep's Clothing

belong to Christ know and respond to His voice.[10] (Henry G. Bosch)

Jesus has a distinctive call that is directed to his flock, to those who claim to be followers and disciples of Christ. The call comes in many forms but carries the same theme:

> "Therefore *go and make disciples* of all nations, *baptizing them* in the name of the Father and of the Son and of the Holy Spirit." (Matthew 28:19)

> "Not everyone who says to me, 'Lord, Lord,' will enter the kingdom of heaven, but only the one who *does the will of my Father* who is in heaven." (Matthew 7:21)

> "Whoever wants to be my disciple must *deny themselves and take up their cross and follow me.*" (Matthew 16:24)

> "To the Jews who had believed him, Jesus said, "If you *hold to my teaching*, you are really my disciples." (John 8:31)

> "By this everyone will know that you are my disciples, if you *love one another.*" (John 13:35)

> "This is to my Father's glory, that you *bear much fruit*, showing yourselves to be my disciples." (John 15:8)

Notice all of the action words that signify Christ's call to his followers: *go, make, baptize, does the will, deny, take up, follow, hold to, love, bear*. Obviously, being a disciple requires more than just acknowledging who Jesus is, believing him, or even agreeing with his words. It also means *following* in his footsteps and *doing* what he says.

In his book *Hearing God*, Dallas Willard stresses the importance of being intentional in how we learn to listen for and recognize God's voice in the midst of the daily din and clamor of life. It is through the context of our circumstances, impressions from the Holy Spirit, and passages from scripture that we can be most certain that God is speaking to us. But like wayward sheep, many choose not to listen for what God has to say or become inwardly and outwardly distracted by other "voices," be they of our culture, our workplace, our circle of friends, or even our own families. As Willard explains, these individuals position themselves in such a way that they reflect Jesus' words in Mark 4: "They may indeed look, but not perceive, and may indeed listen, but not understand." While they may present themselves or make claims to the contrary, their actions speak otherwise:

> If we do not want to be converted from our chosen and habitual ways, if we really want to run our own lives without any interference from God, our very perceptual mechanisms will filter out his voice or twist it to our own purposes.... People who understand and warmly desire to hear God's voice will, by contrast, want to hear it when life is uneventful just as much as they want to hear it when they are facing trouble or big decisions ... our failure to hear his voice when we want to is due to the fact that we do not in general want to hear it, that we want it only when we think we need it.[11]

Imagine if real sheep acted this way toward their master/shepherd. I can envision the conversation:

> Sheep 1: Ya' know, Tom is such a great shepherd. He treats us well, gives us plenty to eat—even leads us beside calm waters at times.
>
> Sheep 2: Yep, Tom's one of the best. I don't know what we'd do without him. And that staff he carries—that's got to be one of those elite models, don't ya' know. But hey, did you hear about Charlie?
>
> Sheep 1: No, what happened?
>
> Sheep 2: I guess a mountain lion came too close to the flock the other day when we were all spread out. Tom tried to warn him, but Charlie wouldn't listen. He must've found a really good patch of clover.

A Wolf in Sheep's Clothing

> Sheep 1: Wow, of all the dumb luck. And his poor wife and kids.
>
> Sheep 2: Yeah, you just never know when your day is comin'.

Clearly, there is great cost and even greater consequences in not following Jesus, yet for those who do, the reward is great. For others, the perceived cost of being a disciple of Jesus is far greater and less inviting, causing them to play out the charade of trying to act like a Christian, but beneath the mask, holding to a different worldview that barely scrapes the surface of true discipleship. Dallas Willard describes these double-minded people as having a "reality problem." They lack knowledge at the worldview level. And because they are "on again, off again" in terms of their knowledge of God's acting on their behalf by his will, they are unable to receive what they are asking for.

> One day or hour they are asking God for wisdom, and the next day or hour they are relying on themselves or others. While they are asking God, they have in the corner of their mind the thought that God isn't going to give them what they need, so they must take care of themselves. They are really relying on two different and incompatible things. And when they are trying to get wisdom on their own, they are thinking about the possibility of God giving it to them. On both sides they are undercut by their inner uncertainty about the reliability of God and God's goodwill toward them.[12]

If we truly want to shed our sheep costumes and live honestly before God and man, then we must actively seek serious inward change, cultivating holy habits that will enable us to clearly recognize and hear our Shepherd's voice. It also means that we take spiritual inventory of how well-grounded our hearts and minds are in the ways of God. Consider the following from *Hearing God*:

> When trouble comes, . . . how long does it take us to get around to bringing it to God in prayer? . . . When we are alone, do we constantly recognize that God is present with

us? Does our mind spontaneously return to God when not intensely occupied? ... Our answers to these questions make us sadly aware of how our mind is solidly trained in false ways.[13]

Take Off the Mask

In today's culture, the notion of sin is a foreign concept for many. Even among Christians and in many churches, the theme of "sinners saved by grace" is given a casual nod, if even mentioned at all. Brennan Manning suggests that many of us practice the charade of pretending to believe that we are sinners. As a result, we can only "pretend to believe we have been forgiven." Subsequently, our entire spiritual existence becomes one of "pseudo-repentance and pseudo-bliss."[14] As sin is cheapened, so is grace, and ultimately, so is genuine, authentic Christianity. "The greatest single cause of atheism in the world today is Christians," says Manning, "who acknowledge Jesus with their lips, walk out the door, and deny Him by their lifestyle. That is what an unbelieving world simply finds unbelievable."[15]

So let's stop pretending. Today. Now. Ask yourself: How well do I recognize the call of the Shepherd? Do I heed his voice? Am I "branded" with the mark of his Holy Spirit so that others would know to whom I belong? What is the evidence of this? What place do prayer and scripture reading have in my daily communication with God?

Is my life bearing fruit of any kind? If not, why not?

What sins am I trying to hide with "sheep's clothing"? Or am I hiding beneath the guise of a dutiful sheep dog, filling my life with master-pleasing activities but underneath filled with sloth, pride, or lust? Who am I really trying to deceive?

Is what I wear in public different from what I wear when no one (I think) is watching? What does my answer tell me about myself?

What tangible steps do I need to take to honestly claim Jesus as "Lord"?

A Wolf in Sheep's Clothing

If you begin to answer these questions honestly, you will be well on your way to living the righteous, Spirit-filled life Jesus promised to those who believe and who obey his commandments. As opposed to keeping Jesus in a box on your closet shelf, you will daily commit yourself to following the Master Shepherd, inviting him to lead you and listening to his voice while tuning out the competing voices of this world.

Whoever claims to live in him must live as Jesus did. (**1 John 2:6**)

Hypocrites in the Church? Yes, and in the lodge and at the home. Don't hunt through the Church for a hypocrite. Go home and look in the mirror. Hypocrites? Yes. See that you make the number one less. (Billy Sunday)

Chapter 6:
Fashion: In One Year and Out the Other
(Adapting to the Culture)

> Christians must adapt to the changed cultural circumstance by finding a way "to live faithfully in a world in which we're going to be a moral exception." (Albert Mohler)

> Our call is to an engaged alienation, a Christianity that preserves the distinctiveness of our gospel while not retreating from our callings as neighbors, and friends, and citizens. (Russell Moore)

Every generation—perhaps every decade—is known by three things: major historical events, music, and fashion styles. For me, growing up through the sixties into the seventies, bell-bottom pants, silk shirts with huge collars, and platform shoes became the rage. Moving into the eighties and my later college years, styles became less influenced by the disco era and settled into more loose, comfortable styles that incorporated activewear (i.e., sweat pants and sweatshirts). This was followed by a "preppie" phase that mimicked Ivy League sensibilities of style. As the times changed, so did the clothing, and by adapting to these changes, you hopefully managed to stay "relevant."

Relevance is also considered when traveling or living abroad as one adopts the dress, language, and cultural mores of the local region. Missionaries in particular will often adopt the native dress of the locals to be more accepted by them. Similarly, they may embrace the local customs and conventions to demonstrate an interest in the culture and its people groups and a desire to "speak the language" of the land. This is in direct contrast to missionaries of old who attempted to "civilize" or de-culturalize the native people groups by having them adopt Anglo morals and values with disastrous results. Such approaches were founded on a superior mindset of Western colonialism, or what is referred to as ethnocentrism (aka "my culture is better than yours"). These methods have been since criticized as being "arrogant, ignorant, and imperialistic... [and] have largely been discarded."[1] Rather, today's missions groups lean more toward indigenous forms of worship, the aim being to "ensure that a given people group's worship entirely reflects its own culture, with as tiny a Western footprint as possible."[2]

A Bridge Too Far?

Today we find a similar attempt by many churches and Christian organizations to attract the local culture by appealing to the prevailing language, styles, and trends. But could there be a danger of the relevance pendulum swinging too far? For example, in an effort to reach the unchurched where they live, work, and play, there are churches now that meet in bars and pubs. Recently, a California church decided to convert a downtown bookstore into a brewery that will serve as a church, with the idea of donating a sizeable percent of the profits to charity.[3] Some preachers have been known to use crude or foul language to appeal to the unchurched. "Less extreme, but now ubiquitous," says pastor Peter Ditzel, "are Christian coffeehouses with preachers who seem more like stand-up comics, Jesus rock concerts, Christian meetings that resemble three-ring circuses with all of their derring-do and acrobatics, and Christian automobile racing."[4] Other churches have held retreats for men with the enticement of beer kegs and guns. While the motive is unquestionable (i.e., reaching others with the Gospel message), do the means justify Paul's statement of becoming all things to all men?

Elliott Clark, writing in *The Gospel Coalition*, suggests that American churches have been utilizing what he refers to as "target-culture-focused ministry" in trying to adapt to the prevailing socio-cultural patterns and customs:

> We've managed to take subcultures and make them the defining narrative for whole communities of faith. It wouldn't take much imagination to envision a NASCAR church or Paleo Diet Bible study. As much as colonialism affected previous generations, one has to wonder how much consumerism drives our own. The former represents cultural imposition, the latter cultural capitulation.[5]

The key question is whether a consumeristic approach to drawing non-believers or seekers of faith ends up watering down the Gospel message at the expense of being relevant. "There is nothing inherently wrong with being fashionable or culturally engaged," says Daniel Threlfall. "There *is* something wrong, however, when cultural adaptation becomes more important than gospel living."[6] In other words, when a church's programs and activities become more central to its identity than its message and ministry to its community, there's a danger of diluting or even disregarding the Gospel's impact on living, loving, and learning as a faith-based community. Such a church can easily turn into an "All flash, no substance" type of existence.

A Bridge Unbuilt

Conversely, and perhaps more common, are "dyed-in-the-wool" approaches to welcoming those outside the faith into our culture of belief. Pastor Stephen Kirk, in his book *Multiply*, states that many churches are willing to allow non-believers to "stumble in as long as they adopt new ways." He adds: "We're willing to have them walk across the bridge into our world, but in lieu of a bridge, who's willing to build one that reaches into theirs?"[7]

Pastor Andy Stanley agrees. "We have given culture a lot of other things to argue with us about—needlessly—that sometimes keep people from ever coming close to church," he says. "There is a shift that has to take place if we are to speak into the culture of a world that needs to know there is a God in Heaven who has invited each person to call Him Father."[8]

Doug Pollock, in his small but impactful book *God Space*, echoes this concern. He reminds us that Jesus' Great Commission to his disciples begins with a simple two-letter word: *Go*. Being willing to engage with others in spiritual conversations means having a willingness to move toward the people God has placed in our lives. "I have learned that the best spiritual conversations usually occur in places where others feel comfortable," says Pollock. "The church, on the other hand, communicates to the world, 'If you come to us, we'll listen to you—in our buildings, on our timetable, if you use our language and dress and act as we do.' The 'come and see' approach of most churches is far from the "go and be" mentality modeled by the church in the book of Acts."[9]

Jesus, of course, was the ultimate bridge builder. As we are reminded in Paul's letter to the Philippians, Jesus—while fully God—

> "Did not consider equality with God something to be used to his own advantage; rather, he made himself nothing by taking the very nature of a servant, being made in *human likeness*. And being found in *appearance as a man*, he humbled himself by becoming obedient to death—even death on a cross!" (Philippians 2:6–8, emphasis added)

Jesus incarnated himself into the world of humanity, shedding the glory of heaven and donning mortal flesh so that he could relate to our standing as those created a "little lower than the angels." He shared in our humanity so that he could both experience and overcome death, and in so doing, earn our freedom from sin's slavery:

> For this reason he had to be made like them, fully human in every way, in order that he might become a merciful and

faithful high priest in service to God, and that he might make atonement for the sins of the people. Because he himself suffered when he was tempted, he is able to help those who are being tempted. (Hebrews 2:17–18)

During his earthly ministry, Jesus did not isolate himself from sinners, nor did he exploit divine swagger in his interactions with everyday people. Rather, he hobnobbed with ordinary people,

> Model[ing] a life of freedom and missional adaptation: eating food, enjoying drinks (even providing really good ones!), attending parties, befriending and, yes, even defending sinners with courageous joy *and* without fear of Gospel compromise. Far from huddling in quarantine, Jesus initiated everyday interactions with a commitment to remove any obstacles to grace the so-called "religious" had constructed—some intentionally, some inadvertently.[10]

Paul's Bridge: Adapting Without Adopting

The Apostle Paul understood this incarnational strategy and incorporated it into his own ministry. Doing so stirred him to make the Gospel message available to as many as possible. In his letter to the church in Corinth, he explained his approach in this way:

> To the Jews I became like a Jew, to win the Jews. To those under the law I became like one under the law (though I myself am not under the law), so as to win those under the law. To those not having the law I became like one not having the law (though I am not free from God's law but am under Christ's law), so as to win those not having the law. To the weak I became weak, to win the weak. I have become all things to all people so that by all possible means I might save some. (1 Corinthians 9:20–22)

Clearly, Paul was in the perfect position to be "all things to all men." As he stated in his oratory before the leaders in Jerusalem, Paul claimed his Jewish ancestry, even speaking to the crowd in Aramaic to substantiate his bloodline. When arrested for speaking out and inciting the Jews, he avowed his Roman citizenry to the centurion in charge of him. When brought before the Jewish Sanhedrin to hear his case, he claimed his affiliation as a former Pharisee, leading to disagreement between the Pharisees and Sadducees. And when addressing Greek philosophers in Athens, he made reference to their religious history and objects of worship. Yes, Paul enjoyed a rich and diverse heritage and upbringing and used it to his advantage when presenting the Gospel message to a melting pot of cultures and worldviews. Moreover,

> Paul was so free in Christ, virtually nothing hindered him from drawing near to those who needed Gospel grace. Prior to meeting Christ, Paul was bound to one set of exclusive traditions—an old dog stubbornly disinclined to new tricks. But having received Gospel grace, Jesus set him free to lovingly participate in all kinds of cultural experiences with a whole cast of "unsightly" characters he might otherwise have avoided.[11]

Like Jesus, though, Paul was careful not to cross the lines of sin when sharing the Gospel. Presenting the Gospel within the context of the culture does not mean that we condone sinful or worldly behavior, but rather, we allow grace to lead us into earnest yet winsome engagement with not-yet-Christians. Unfortunately, many of us as Christians tend to equate our associations with those outside the faith with the very sin God's grace is meant to eradicate or absolve.* Either that or we become so chameleon-like as to be indistinguishable from the culture around us, and in the process, end up watering down the Gospel (and corrupting God's call to holiness).

Stephen Kirk puts it this way:

> In our effort to avoid condoning their choices and lifestyle, perhaps we've forfeited the opportunity to show them acceptance, treating them with the respect creatures made in God's glorious image deserve. The truth is, we all tend

to drift to one of two unhelpful extremes. Some of us err on the *loose* side of being so compromised by the culture that we offer little contrast and thus mute our influence. Others of us err on the *legalistic* side of being so alien and disconnected from the culture that we offer little to no connection and thus similarly no chance at Gospel influence . . . neither pure indulgence nor pure separation is pure Gospel.**[12]

Doug Pollock tells of an experience in which he was asked by a contingent of local churches to address their desire to reach out to their community. At the completion of the workshop, he invited the participants to join him at a local bar to apply what they had learned that day. There were no takers. When asked what their reservations were in doing so, the responses revealed a general consensus that bars were a place for carousing, swearing, drunkenness, and the like. When asked if they would like to see the people at the bar at church on Sunday morning, every hand raised. "Who do you think is going to make the first move?" he asked them. He wondered out loud to the group: "How many bar patrons would be willing to leave their 'club' on a Sunday morning to attend 'your' club to listen to a lengthy talk about a man who lived 2000 years ago and then 'pay' for it when an offering plate is passed?"[13]

Author and pastor Mark Batterson shared a story of a friend who decided to infiltrate the adult film industry with the Gospel and the love of Christ, handing out Bibles at various porn conventions. "If we are going to fulfill our ancient commission," said Batterson, later reflecting on his friend's boldness, "we need to get out of the comfortable confines of our Christian ghettos and invade some hellholes with the light and love of Christ."[14]

Several years ago, I was challenged in a similar way. It was after reading the text in Matthew in which Jesus addresses his disciples about their call to ministry:

> For I was hungry and you gave me something to eat, I was thirsty and you gave me something to drink, I was

> a stranger and you invited me in, I needed clothes and you clothed me, I was sick and you looked after me, I was in prison and you came to visit me.... Truly I tell you, whatever you did for one of the least of these brothers and sisters of mine, you did for me. (Matthew 25:35–36, 40)

Although I had read and heard that passage countless times before, I was convicted by the words, "I was in prison and you came to visit me." Up until that point, I had had no opportunity or even desire to set foot in any type of correctional facility. *Those people belong there for a reason*, I thought. *I'm not feeling particularly called to do that.* But as the Holy Spirit continued to perform his work in me, I gradually became more convinced that this is something I *should* do—that I was *called* to do. Beginning by corresponding with inmates by mail, I gradually worked up to a point that I became involved in mentoring inmates in a short-term correctional facility, helping them to find employment once they were released, while also sharing God's message of hope and grace to each man I visited. Although my visits were typically less than an hour, for that brief time, I was in a sense "imprisoned" with them, temporarily shedding my freedom and personal agenda to step into their world.

Too Heavenly or Too Worldly?

John Piper reminds us that Christ died to set us free from God's wrath and from the loveless limits of the law. Are we using our freedom to make this good news plain, or have we so separated ourselves that we have no connection with unbelievers? On the other hand, are we so worldly that those outside the faith don't know we have anything radically different to offer? Yes, we need to shed the cloak of legalism when engaging our culture; however, that does not mean we engage in unbiblical or sinful practices for the sake of the Gospel. So how do we avoid either extreme?

To circumvent the latter *permissive* stance, Piper suggests that we keep vigilant watch over our hearts to ensure we are remaining in the law of Christ. He suggests two self-reflective questions:

Fashion: In One Year and Out the Other

1. Are you becoming more worldly-minded than they are becoming spiritually-minded? If so, you have probably crossed the line of the law of Christ. Christ does not call you to lose your holiness, but to gain theirs.

2. Is your passion for winning your friends and family growing, or is it shrinking as you become all things to them? If it is shrinking, then you are not in the law of Christ at that point.[15]

Conversely, to avoid becoming legalistic in our approach to non-Christians, we can seek to become more intentional in our interactions. Stephen Kirk suggests that some of us need to essentially let go of some of our hang-ups about participating in certain social activities or "negotiables," as Paul alludes to in his letter to the Romans. Just as Jesus had no qualms about spending time with riff-raff and the castoffs of society, so should we be willing to place ourselves in socially uncomfortable situations for the sake of others experiencing Gospel grace, maybe for the first time. In taking stock of our own personal bent for sharing the Gospel,

> Some of us need to be freer to participate in common cultural practices that might actually open doors to future disciples, whereas others of us need to *abstain* from certain practices that keep future disciples from even knowing there's a door.[16]

Obviously, most of us do not possess Paul's pedigree or have not been subject to such a varied and wide-ranging array of experiences as he was. Quite frankly, many of us are hesitant simply to share our faith story with others because we're afraid of offending them or acting as if we're trying to "win them over" to our side. True, there may be some who will take offense at what the Gospel has to say, but it doesn't mean that we have to be offensive in our approach. Penn Jillette, self-acknowledged atheist and part of the Las Vegas comedy-illusionist team of Penn and Teller, once had a man approach him after one of his performances. The man complimented Jillette on the show and then handed him a pocket New Testament. After sharing some friendly conversation, the entertainer later reflected on this exchange:

> I've always said that I don't respect people who don't proselytize. I don't respect that at all. If you believe that there's a heaven and a hell, and people could be going to hell or not getting eternal life, and you think that it's not really worth telling them this because it would make it socially awkward ... how much do you have to hate somebody to *not* proselytize? How much do you have to hate somebody to believe everlasting life is possible and not tell them that? I mean, if I believed, beyond the shadow of a doubt, that a truck was coming at you, and you didn't believe that truck was bearing down on you, there is a certain point where I tackle you. And this is *more* important than that.[17]

We also may have reservations about sharing our faith because of any number of perceived inadequacies on our part. "I'm not gifted in that area," we may claim. "That's the job of pastors," we might decide, or "I wouldn't have the right answers" we could confess. Yet God, in his infinite wisdom, matches our particular character traits, life events, and skill sets to engage with the people he places in our path. It is no accident that you live in the neighborhood or community that you do. It is scarcely by chance that you earn your living in the particular work place in which you are employed. And coincidence has nothing to do with the "random" conversation you have with the checkout clerk at Target, your barber or hairstylist, or the guys in your golf foursome. God orchestrates our encounters with other individuals in ways we can't and don't fathom, yet we must begin seeing these "God space" moments as real opportunities to share Gospel grace, becoming watchful and intentional in stewarding our time toward faith encounters.

Doug Pollock proposes that one of the best ways to engage people and incarnate into your surrounding culture is to "wonder" your way into spiritual conversations. In this sense, questions are more important than giving theologically correct answers. More specifically, "Wondering questions tap into a reservoir of curiosity that lies deep within each of us." As a result, we can rid ourselves of any notion that we need to have all the answers. Opening ourselves to the possibility of inquisitive inquiry and wonder with another can lead to a number of positive outcomes:

- A climate of mutual curiosity in which we explore the mystery of life together, as fellow sojourners
- A tearing down of the "us-versus-them" wall
- The possibility of mutual discovery
- The elimination of the fear factor that keeps most Christ-followers from actively participating in spiritual conversations[18]

This built-in inquisitiveness is why Jesus said that anyone who took the time to seek and ask would find (Matthew 7:7) and that those who knocked, the door would be opened to them (Luke 11:9). We can begin the conversation by asking open-ended questions in which "*our* wonder stimulates *their* wonder and paves the way for spiritual conversations to flow naturally. Effective wondering starts where people are, not where we'd like them to be," says Pollock. "When we wonder out loud with people about what's important to them . . . we create an open, safe, and nonjudgmental forum for authentic dialogue."[19] Doing so helps others search and discover new revelations on their own without feeling manipulated (which only "communicates disrespect and stifle[s] the supernatural allure of the kingdom").

What About Apologetics?

In Christian theology, apologetics refers to any reasoned attempts to defend Christianity against objections. While apologetics may still have some relevance in this post-modern/post-Christian culture, it should not be the first or primary approach when sharing the Gospel. Nor should it be abandoned totally. Many will argue that Paul's defense of the faith to the Jews and Greeks in Athens amounted to apologetics or informed debate. However, the results of his reasoning were mixed—some listeners sneered while others followed.

Most people who like to listen to and debate ideas aren't seeking to have their minds changed. And while there are some who have come to the faith as a result of intelligent debate or discourse with a believer, the primary catalyst for igniting one's faith journey lies in relationship. It's less about drubbing someone with facts about the Christian faith and more about what Lee Strobel calls "relational apologetics." "It's [about] friendships," he says. "It's conversations. It's dialogue where we engage with these questions, these topics on a personal level. It doesn't just become, 'Golly, why does a loving God allow pain and suffering?' It becomes, 'Where was God when we lost a child in childbirth five years ago?'"[20]

When others know that we are genuinely interested in them as people and accept them where they are, then we come across as less intimidating and our words are given more credibility. When we go heavy on "proving" the legitimacy of the Gospel, we risk coming across as appearing superior or as trying to win the debate, making the act of listening secondary to our conversations. While we should be committed to being "prepared to give an answer for why our hope is in Christ" (1 Peter 3:15), people should be drawn to us with questions about the hope that we have. Indeed, we need to prove the basis for this hope, but ultimately, love is our proof.[21]

As for the mandate to proclaim the Gospel, Jesus is never clearer than when he tells his disciples, "Whoever publicly acknowledges me before others, the Son of Man will also acknowledge before the angels of God. But whoever disowns me before others will be disowned before the angels of God" (Luke 12:8–9). And if we lack confidence in our ability to come up with the right words, Jesus offered the following encouragement: "When you are brought before synagogues, rulers and authorities, do not worry about how you will defend yourselves or what you will say, for the Holy Spirit will teach you at that time what you should say" (Luke 12:11–12). At the very least, we can learn to contextualize our message to mirror our culture and speak in ways others can understand. Using language, metaphors, humor, and illustrations that resonate with our audience can help us to adapt our Gospel presentation to a particular group or individual outside the faith. The Holy Spirit will take care of the rest.

Adapt or Become Irrelevant

In a metaphorical yet practical sense, many of us need to change or adapt our "clothing" to stay relevant with our culture. Some of us have adopted monastic clothing by isolating ourselves from the culture (choosing to remain cloistered within our own little "churchy" groups). Some of us wear clothing that no one can relate to (reaching out but speaking a strange language of "Christianese" with those outside the faith). Still others prefer to wear an "invisibility cloak" (à *la* Harry Potter) in which we are present but hidden within the culture. (Their motto: Just don't ask me about my faith.) Finally, some are so fashion conscious that it's more about the "clothes"—about appearances—than about the message.

Ask yourself the following questions. Go ahead—do it right now:

- What stumbling blocks have you (or your church) placed in the way of future Christ followers? How have you expected others to join you on *your* terms when preparing to share the good news? Have you contrived any "deal breakers" when it comes to sharing the Gospel (e.g., declaring settings or situations *verboten* for having conversations about faith)? Remember who Jesus associated with and where that often took him.

- Paul was compelled by Christ's otherworldly saving love, "yielding personal preference to the greater goal of spreading the blessing of Gospel grace."[22] Are you so compelled and if not, why? What personal comfort zones are you willing to step out of to connect with someone outside the faith but within your reach?

- Who are some individuals within your circle of influence with whom you can begin having "wondering" conversations? What are some "wondering" questions that could initiate and stimulate these conversations?

- "Even if you're not sure all that it will mean, are you at least willing to ask King Jesus to lead you into incarnational living?"[23] This is often the first step and affirms your willingness to embrace Jesus' command to "go and make disciples."

Asking yourself and honestly responding to these questions will obviously mean taking some risks, but go ahead. Make the effort to adapt your "fashion" to the culture around you that's within your realm of influence. If you stick a toe into the water, you'll find the temperature isn't all that bad. And pretty soon, the feet, legs, and whole body will follow—submerged in God's grace and emboldened by the Holy Spirit to offer a hand or word of encouragement to someone who is in over his or her head but is desperately wanting to be rescued.

> The graced are indeed the best and only conduits of grace. (Stephen Kirk)
>
> Learning and innovation go hand in hand. The arrogance of success is to think that what you did yesterday will be sufficient for tomorrow. (William Pollard)

---

*One study has shown that the longer a person is a Christian, the fewer friends he or she has outside the faith.

**I once heard a youth pastor talk of evangelizing someone who happened to be a smoker. In order to meet him halfway, he smoked a pack of cigarettes with this person even though he himself was not a smoker. Obviously, smoking for some is a gray area not directly addressed in the Bible. However, did this youth pastor compromise his convictions in any way to reach this unchurched individual? Or could he have approached this situation differently?

Chapter 7:
Dressed for Battle—Part One
(This Means War!)

> Finally, be strong in the Lord and in his mighty power. Put on the full armor of God, so that you can take your stand against the devil's schemes. (Ephesians 6:10–11)

> There will be no danger which may not be successfully met by the power of God; nor will any who, with this assistance [the armor of God], fight against Satan, fail in the day of battle. (John Calvin)

It's amazing the things you can discover from a simple internet search. For example, there happens to be several websites that specialize in selling medieval garb, primarily for the purpose of battle reenactments. As one website states:

> Get Dressed For Battle, also known as GDFB, has been gaining popularity in Europe over the years as the number one supplier of affordable, functional garments and armour for reenactment and combat use. We're offering a wide range of GDFB products and adding more every day. Get Dressed For Battle is a company that makes the widest

selection of chainmail, helmets, armour, and medieval garments in the world. Each GDFB product is professionally made and fully functional for its intended use and will make a hit at your next medieval get together or Ren fair. Choose your armour, helmets, or chainmail and GET DRESSED FOR BATTLE![1]

Who knew? Yet, reenactments of famous battles are a favorite pastime for many aficionados of certain periods in history (medieval or Civil War come to mind). While such reenactments are often based on actual events and faithfully attempt to capture the spirit and authenticity of the time, these events are all usually done in a spirit of goodwill with opposing "forces" often shaking hands or sharing other forms of camaraderie at the end of the mock battle. Nevertheless, the "reenactors" take great pains to replicate the uniforms, weapons, and combat that were common to that particular historical period.

As Christians we, too, are engaged in a "reenactment" of sorts—one that is playing out on an earthly battlefield while simultaneously occurring in the heavenly realms. As described by Paul in Ephesians 6:

> For our struggle is not against flesh and blood, but against the rulers, against the authorities, against the powers of this dark world and against the spiritual forces of evil in the heavenly realms. (Ephesians 6:12)

This is no mere reproduction or simulation of a real-world historical battle (although the war itself has been played out for millennia). "Wars on earth are but tremors felt from an earthquake light-years away," writes John White. "The Christian's war takes place at the epicenter of the earthquake. It is infinitely more deadly, while the issues that hang on it make earth's most momentous questions no more than village gossip."[2]

The battle that Paul refers to is a spiritual one—an "other" world type of skirmish. While Paul uses the analogy of a Roman soldier's armor, the symbolism implies that a more spiritual, unworldly force

Dressed for Battle—Part One

is at work. And in the context of non-earthly dimensions, one would assume that typical warfare and weaponry would not suffice.

Paul's use of the word *struggle* in his letter to the Ephesians refers to the Greek word *palē*, meaning to engage in hand-to-hand fighting or to wrestle. In our struggle with the "spiritual forces of evil," we must call on all of our available strength and resources to defend and protect our souls. The notion that "Satan is alive and well" is no less true than it was in Paul's time, and perhaps more so. But regardless of the moment in time, Satan seems to employ the same motives in this battle for control over our souls. According to Kay Arthur, the Enemy has three objectives as he engages with each of us individually:

- To destroy our unity with God, the body of Christ, and our families.
- To entice us to sin so that he can gain a place in our lives as children of God.
- To lead us into false teaching.[3]

With much at stake in the battle against satanic powers, the Apostle Paul, using the images of his time, proposed that followers of Christ arm themselves for spiritual warfare much like a Roman soldier (the foreign oppressors of Paul's day). The imagery of Paul's words in Ephesians 6 no doubt made a huge impact on his readers. Given the lay of the political landscape of the time, the Jewish nation resented but had grown accustomed to the presence of the Roman army in their midst. And while imprisoned for nearly two years under Roman authority, Paul undoubtedly had close contact with many guards who wore the standard armor of the day. The various pieces of the armor "suit"—the breastplate, belt, helmet, etc.—projected an imposing presence, one that asserted control, power, and influence. The Jewish nation, while allowed to maintain their culture and religion, likely felt like puppets under Rome's strong rule.

Knowing the struggles that the young church was experiencing (political as well as religious persecution), Paul painted a visual picture that the believers at Ephesus could both relate to and be encouraged by:

> Therefore put on the full armor of God, so that when the day of evil comes, you may be able to stand your ground, and after you have done everything, to stand. Stand firm then, with the belt of truth buckled around your waist, with the breastplate of righteousness in place, and with your feet fitted with the readiness that comes from the gospel of peace. In addition to all this, take up the shield of faith, with which you can extinguish all the flaming arrows of the evil one. Take the helmet of salvation and the sword of the Spirit, which is the word of God. (Ephesians 6:13–17)

Let's explore the armor Paul mentioned in greater detail and see what implications it has for us in the 21st century.

The Armor of God

In his book *Dressed to Kill*, Rick Renner provides a vivid description of the armor typically worn by Roman soldiers of the time. It is estimated that the total mass of a full body of armor most likely weighed in at about 100 pounds, so the average-sized soldier no doubt needed to be strong and physically fit. In addition to wearing the loinbelt, breastplate, shoes, and helmet, Roman soldiers also wielded a protective shield, as well as weapons of combat such as a sword and often a lance. Collectively, it is hard to fathom carrying this load into battle, often over miles of terrain. Yet the Roman army was a force with which to be reckoned, a well-oiled machine in its day that struck fear in the hearts of many of its foes.

As for the specific pieces of armor, Renner provides the following brief descriptions:

- **Loinbelt**—the least impressive but central piece of armor that held all other pieces together; it mainly held the breastplate in place while the shield and sword attached to the belt on clips.

Dressed for Battle—Part One

- **Breastplate**—essentially two large sheets of metal front and back, the heaviest piece covering the bottom of the neck to the waist or below.
- **Shoes**—these included a *greave*, which wrapped around the soldier's lower legs, and the boot itself, which usually incorporated spikes on the bottom sole.
- **Shield**—made of multiple layers of animal hide and then framed along the edges by a strong piece of metal or wood.
- **Helmet**—this obviously protected a soldier from a fatal blow to the head and could weigh 15 pounds or more.
- **Sword**—often a very heavy, broad, and massive weapon with two sharp edges designed for jabbing and killing.
- **Lance**—although not specifically mentioned by Paul, it could be implied as part of the whole armor that a Roman soldier typically carried.[4]

Many of us are unfamiliar with a suit of armor in the present age as it became defunct several hundred years ago with the advent of artillery and the impracticality and cost of armor. But perhaps a modern day comparison will bring things to light.

The Marvel Comics fictional hero Iron Man is the creation of Tony Stark—genius inventor and billionaire owner of a technology company bearing his name. Having made much of his fortune designing weapons for the military, Stark was kidnapped one day by terrorists who wanted him to build a weapon of mass destruction. Rather than comply with the terrorists' wishes, Stark secretly built a suit of armor that allowed him to escape his captors. As his alter ego—Iron Man—Tony Stark became invincible, using his suit to not only escape but also to later fight evil and injustice in the world. While defenseless outside of the suit, inside his hi-tech armor, Stark became essentially invulnerable.[5]

While we may not battle terrorists or super-villains in a high-tech suit of armor (if you do, I won't give away your identity), as

Christians we are engaged in a battle that requires a certain level of protection—a spiritual suit of armor that makes us invincible against our enemy if we use it.

T. D. Jakes states that every piece of armor pertains to our identity in Christ, each mirroring a spiritual truth about who we are in Christ. And while battle armor covered the Roman soldier from head to toe, our spiritual armor permeates and purifies our entire being.[6] Let's take a closer look at each of these pieces of armor to learn more about their actual and spiritual significance in the context of Paul's passage.

The Belt of Truth

As a boy, I loved reading the superhero comic books at the barbershop. One of my favorite superheroes was Batman who, in retrospect, had no real super powers. Instead, his "powers" came from a variety of high-tech weapons, ranging from his Batmobile to the Batcopter to the tools on his utility belt. Interestingly, Wikipedia has its own page dedicated to Batman's utility belt, including a list of 30-plus items that have appeared on this super-belt. There was no situation, no villain for which Batman didn't have some tool at his disposal to ward off the attacks of his enemies.[7]

Upon inspection of the Roman soldier's battle wear, the loinbelt (compared to Batman's wide array of belt tools) may at first glance seem like an insignificant piece of armor. However, it was actually central—even integral—to keeping the rest of the soldier's armor in place and connected. It also served more as a girdle than a belt in terms of its protective properties, surrounding the lower torso and providing critical support during battle. As such, it was important for the Roman warrior to have a strong and protected "core" when facing his adversaries. Similarly, the believer's belt of truth or core serves an important function. If by truth we mean God's truth—what is true in his Word, his promises, and his character—then having our life dependent on a strong core is critical to our survival as Christians.

Dressed for Battle—Part One

As Priscilla Shirer points out in her book *The Armor of God*, many workout programs fail to address the *core*, which refers to all the muscles in the abdominal area that are responsible for functional strength and stability. Having a strong or well-developed core is important as it "helps with your balance, your stability, your resistance to injury, your stamina over time and under pressure ... the condition of your core affects everything."[8] Representing then God's Word or Truth, having a weak or limited core (or understanding of the truth) sets you up for attacks and leaves you vulnerable to the lies and deception that the enemy sends your way. Holding fast to the truth—to God's Word—is your core support, providing the necessary backing needed when in the midst of battle. Unless you know what is true at your core, then you leave yourself exposed and defenseless to Satan's attacks.

What are signs of a weak core? Shirer points to at least three indicators:

1. Poor Posture—If your core is weak, then you are more likely to buckle under the pressure of carrying heavy loads (emotional as well as physical). By comparison, a strong core helps you to stand straighter and more aligned for longer periods of time.

2. Injury Prone—Because the core muscles hold the spine in place, any weakness in this area will destabilize the backbone during strenuous activity, making it more susceptible to injury. This can potentially impact your whole system. Relationally, you may choose to allow others' words or actions to wound you rather than offering grace and forgiveness. When you allow anger or bitterness to get the best of you, you are actually misled into believing distorted facts and a skewed perception of the truth of who God is and who you are in him.

3. Body Fatigue—An unsupported core can sap your energy level needed for other body systems to work efficiently. Similarly, when not girded by God's truth, your relationship with him becomes lackluster, tiresome, and unfulfilling, which in turn seeps into other areas of your life.[9]

Kevin Vanhoozer, professor of systematic theology at Trinity Evangelical Divinity School, speaks of theological core training wherein "our core identity involves core beliefs (believing God's Word), core choices (obeying God's Word), and core relationships (indwelling God's Word)." To strengthen this core means to "attend diligently to the convictions, choices, and relationships that define us, all of which involve attending and responding to the Word of God."[10]

Conversely, when you "ignore the Word of God and cease to apply it to your life on a daily basis, you have willfully chosen to let your entire spiritual life come apart at the seams."[11] Over time, your spiritual compass (your true sense of what constitutes righteousness, peace, and joy) becomes uncalibrated, your faith weakens, and your spiritual core begins to crumble. What used to protect you from the enemy's attacks will now allow you to easily succumb to the lies and deception—the *untruths*—that Satan has at his disposal.

"The Bible," says Renner, "must be the governor, the law, the ruler, and the final say-so in your life. If you don't have the loinbelt of truth firmly positioned in your life, you will not be able to experientially walk in the other pieces of weaponry God has given you."[12] As Kay Arthur points out, just as the soldier's belt kept everything in place and connected, so does truth keep everything in its proper place, helping believers know right from wrong. And being exposed to and regularly immersed in the truth assures that our belts are tightened and ready for action. "If you aren't actively reading the Bible, absorbing it, studying it," says Arthur, "you won't be convinced of its truth. Truth must become at home in you, and you must be at home in it. Otherwise, you'll find it easy to diminish it or to add to it."[13] Put another way, the more you get into God's Word, the more it gets into you.

Additionally, the loinbelt had the capacity to protect and preserve a soldier's ability to reproduce. As such, our relationship with God's Word has direct bearing on our ability to bear fruit. In a sense, we can become spiritually "sterile" if we are not actively involving

God's Word in our lives. Ultimately, we can be reduced to a state of spiritual barrenness.[14]

So how do we put on the belt of truth? Priscilla Shirer offers the following suggestions:

- You uphold and affirm the standard—the truth and boundaries set by God in Scripture. You commit yourself to them and resolve to teach them to your family.

- You daily, systematically, repeatedly begin letting God help you align your decisions and responses, even your attitudes and ambitions, alongside his benchmark of truth.

- You continually learn about the character and purposes of God—both from the Bible and from his Spirit. Then you unapologetically synchronize your convictions, even when you find it hard or unpopular to do so.

- You filter every circumstance, personally and culturally, through the prism of his Word instead of merely leaning on your feelings, political correctness, or the opinions of others.[15]

The Breastplate of Righteousness

The Roman soldier's breastplate was a crucial piece of armor, mainly due to its defensive function in protecting the wearer's vital organs—namely, the heart. A direct hit or penetration to the chest wall could mean the difference between life and death. Thus, its size and bulk were intentionally designed to provide the greatest barrier between the soldier's torso and the enemy's weapons.

Rick Renner describes the breastplate that the Roman soldiers wore as the shiniest, most elaborate piece of armor. Other than the soldier's shield, it provided the most coverage and protection of any of the pieces of armor, often covering from the top of the neck down to the knees in some cases. Two solid pieces of metal (front and back) were attached at the shoulders with thick brass rings. In all, the breastplate ensemble could weigh as much as forty pounds. Oftentimes the large sheets of metal comprised smaller pieces resembling fish scales. As the Roman soldier moved, the pieces of metal rubbed together, causing them to become shinier over time. In the sun, it took on a dazzling appearance as the sun's rays reflected off of the shiny scales. A platoon of Roman soldiers made quite an impression on a sunny day! As such, the breastplate could serve an offensive purpose by blinding the eyes of the enemy.[16]

As a symbol of our righteousness as Christians, our breastplates must be worn daily in recognition of God's gift through our faith in Christ. Jesus, after all, gave up his rights to make us right with God. As Paul reminds us:

> God made him who had no sin to be sin for us, so that in him we might become the righteousness of God. (2 Corinthians 5:21)

> But now apart from the law the righteousness of God has been made known, to which the Law and the Prophets testify. This righteousness is given through faith in Jesus Christ to all who believe. (Romans 3:21–22)

> For if, by the trespass of the one man, death reigned through that one man, how much more will those who receive God's abundant provision of grace and of the gift of righteousness reign in life through the one man, Jesus Christ! (Romans 5:17)

Renner points out that "the more you wear your breastplate of righteousness, walking through life fully conscious of your righteousness in Christ, the more brightly you will shine as a light in a dark world of sin. And as you walk with your breastplate firmly in place, you will learn that your righteousness is not only a defensive weapon to protect you from the blow of the enemy, but it is also an offensive weapon to assist you as you assault the enemy and take back lost territory!"[17]

Diversionary Tactics

The fact is, our adversary Satan wants to convince us that as Christians, we are not righteous in Christ. He searches for those who do not know the truth of God's bestowed righteousness on his children, aiming for and attacking our vitals—the very heart of our beliefs.

Priscilla Shirer examines this further by revealing the heart to be composed of various elements: our mind (thoughts), our will (ambition), our emotions (feelings), and our conscience (moral compass). Satan's battle plan is to attack on one or more of these levels of your heart, waging battle against your:

- **Mind**—by distorting your thinking with lies about God, his Word, and even yourself, trying to cripple your soul through negative, unbiblical thought processes.

- **Will**—by redirecting your ambitions away from eternal, godly pursuits luring you toward interests that are temporal, short-sighted, even directly opposed to the will of God.

- **Emotions**—by tampering with your feelings, piggybacking on runaway responses such as anger, discouragement, revenge, or sadness to persuade you into making unstable choices.

- **Conscience**—by influencing your conscience so it steers you to live in a way that doesn't line up with biblical guidelines.[18]

Taking each of these areas separately, let's examine some specific ways in which Satan could render us vulnerable and how we can use truth effectively as a defensive measure.

Attacks of the Mind

The most notable example of Satan attempting to distort God's truth or distort his Word can be found at the beginning of Jesus' ministry. As cited in chapter 4 of Matthew's gospel, Jesus was led into the desert by the Spirit to be tempted by the devil. What made Jesus particularly vulnerable to attack was the fact that he had fasted forty days and nights prior to this event. As such, Jesus was no doubt experiencing extreme hunger, not to mention feeling physically weak and fatigued. Satan sought to take advantage of Jesus' weakened state from the get-go.

"If you are the Son of God," Satan said to Jesus, "then command these stones to become loaves of bread." Knowing that Jesus was fully capable of performing such a feat, Satan wanted to see if God's Son would take the bait. Jesus, though, being himself the Word and Truth personified, hoisted up his own belt of truth in reply: "Man shall not live by bread alone, but by every word that comes from the mouth of God." Jesus 1, Satan 0.

Satan tried another tactic. He took Jesus to the top of the temple, the highest manmade structure in Jerusalem, and told him, "If you are really the Son of God, throw yourself down, for it is written, 'He will command his angels concerning you,' and 'On their hands they will bear you up, lest you strike your foot against a stone.'"

Jesus, knowing scripture inside and out, replied: "It is also written, 'You shall not put the Lord your God to the test.'" *Is that all you got?* he may have been thinking. *Your words against mine? C'mon, Lucifer. Bring it on!* Jesus 2, Satan 0.

Finally, Satan pulled out all his punches and went for the jugular. Taking Jesus to a mountain top, he gestured toward the grand view before them—all the kingdoms of the world in all their glory. "See all this?" Satan exclaimed. "This could all be yours if you will simply bow down and worship me." Jesus had had enough. "Beat it, Satan!" He backed his rebuke with a third quotation from Deuteronomy: "Worship the Lord your God, and only him. Serve him with absolute single-heartedness" (MSG). With that, it was game over. The home team soundly beat their opponent 3–0. Satan left licking his wounds while Jesus was cared for by angels.

In a similar vein, Satan tries to attack Jesus' followers by distorting truths (even turning biblical passages on their heads) and feeding our minds with subtle half-truths and outright lies in an attempt to make us succumb to his wily ways. While they number many, what follows are some common lies and distortions that the enemy often resorts to (with countering scripture in bold):

- The Bible is fallible because it was written by men, is culturally irrelevant, is outdated, (fill in the blank) . . . therefore, we can disregard what it says or pick and choose which passages are relevant to us. **"All Scripture is God-breathed and is useful for teaching, rebuking, correcting and training in righteousness."** (2 Timothy 3:16)

- There are many ways to God, so just pick the one that best fits. **"I am the way and the truth and the life. No one comes to the Father except through me."** (John 14:6)

- You go to church on occasion, pay your taxes, volunteer, and are basically a good person so you're in like flint in God's eyes. **"There is no one righteous, not even one . . . righteousness is given through faith in Jesus Christ to all who believe. There is no difference between Jew and Gentile, for all have sinned and fall short of the glory of God, and all are justified freely by his grace through the redemption that came by Christ Jesus."** (Romans 3:10, 22–24)

- You're not as bad as a mass murderer or a sexual predator, so God will overlook your "little" sins. **"As it is, you boast in your arrogant schemes. All such boasting is evil. If anyone, then, knows the good they ought to do and doesn't do it, it is sin for them."** (James 4:16–17)

- You deserve to have a little fun once in awhile—after all, you don't want to be known as a prude or holier-than-thou person. **"As He who called you *is* holy, you also be holy in all *your* conduct, because it is written, 'Be holy, for I am holy.'"** (1 Peter 1:15–16)*

Attacks of the Will

Another ploy Satan uses to bring us down is to attack our will or to lead us away from God's will. While believers who are growing in Christ seek to discover and accomplish God's will in their lives, the ways of the flesh under the manipulation of Satan's schemes often misdirect godly ambitions in selfish or less than godly ways. *Thy will be done* often becomes *My will be done*. A common lie with which the enemy tries to trip us is for us to declare what we want to accomplish for God and asking him to approve it without seeking to discover if that is truly what God has in mind for his purposes. Instead, we need to spend time discovering what God is already doing and to join him in that venture.

In his book *Experiencing God,* Henry Blackaby provides us with some valuable insight for discerning whether our will aligns with God's. First of all, we must acknowledge that God is at work all around us while also pursuing a loving relationship with all of his children. Because of this, he invites us to join with him in his work. Through the workings of the Holy Spirit, God reveals himself, his purposes, and his ways through *scripture, prayer, circumstances in our lives, and the church*. Additionally, God's invitation to engage in his work often results in a crisis of belief that must be resolved through faith and action and by making major adjustments in our lives to join God in what he is doing. Finally, we come to know God's will by experience as we obey him and he accomplishes his work through us.[19]

Scripture abounds with accounts of God's people seeking after their own will rather than God's. In 1 Samuel 4, for example, the Israelites mistakenly assumed that by taking the Ark of the Covenant into battle with them against the Philistines, their victory over the enemy would be secured. Instead of seeking God's guidance, they based their confidence in the symbol of the Ark. Subsequently, the presence of the Ark only served to strengthen the Philistines' resolve, allowing them to defeat the Israelites and capture the Ark in the process. King David, too, violated God's will as declared in his laws. To cover up his adulterous relationship with Bathsheba, wife of Uriah, David sent her husband to the front lines of battle so that he would be killed in action. Rather than honoring God's will regarding the sanctity of human life and marital relations, David followed his own sinful will, leading to unintended but avoidable moral failings. Needless to say, when the Enemy attacks our wills, we generally suffer the consequences in the end.

Dressed for Battle—Part One

Attacks of the Emotions

When it comes to our belief in God, feelings are not entirely reliable as barometers of our faith. Satan knows this and will do his level best to play on our feelings. It is not uncommon for Christians, even long-time believers, to experience a wide range of emotions in response to personal crises, setbacks, and failures. For some, it is not unusual for individuals with strong faith to experience what is often referred to as "wilderness" moments—times in which God seems silent, absent, or detached. Accompanying feelings of despair, loneliness, and alienation can feed into our thinking that God has abandoned us or no longer has our best interests in mind.

The late Bill Bright, founder of Campus Crusade for Christ, often referred to the "train" analogy when describing the link between fact, faith, and feelings:

> Do not depend upon feelings. Tied as they are to your ever-changing circumstances, feelings are unreliable in evaluating your relationship with God. The unchanging promises of God's Word, not your feelings, are your authority. The Christian is to live by faith, trusting in the trustworthiness of God Himself and His Word. A train is a good illustration of the relationship between fact, faith, and feeling.

> Let us call the train engine "fact"—the fact of God's promises found in his Word. The fuel car we will call "faith"—your trust in God and his Word. The caboose we will call "feelings."

> As fuel flows into the engine, the train runs. It would be futile and, of course, ridiculous to attempt to pull the train by the caboose. In the same way you, as a Christian, should not depend upon feelings or emotions to live a Spirit-filled life. Rather, God wants you to simply place your faith in his trustworthiness and the promises of his Word.

Feelings are like the caboose—they are important but are designed to follow a life of faith and obedience. Jesus promised all who obey Him, "Whoever has my commands and obeys them, he is the one who loves me. He who loves me will be loved by my Father, and I too will love him and show myself to him." So, you can expect to have a valid emotional relationship with our Lord when you trust and obey Him. But you should never depend on feelings or seek after an emotional experience. The very act of looking for an emotional experience is a denial of the concept of faith, and whatever is not of faith is sin.[20]

Attacks of the Conscience

On that fateful day of September 11, 2001—chiseled into the memories of all Americans and the world, for that matter—terrorists hijacked four separate commercial domestic aircraft for the purpose of committing acts of violence on American soil. Three of the planes reached their destination—two crashing into the Twin Towers of New York City's World Trade Center, ultimately disintegrating both buildings, and the other crashing into the western section of the Pentagon. The fourth aircraft, while also hijacked and commandeered by terrorists, did not reach its intended destination (thought to be either the White House or the United States Capitol). Rather, a group of brave passengers attempted to wrest control of the plane from the hijackers, resulting in the untimely death of all aboard in a rural field in Pennsylvania. A memorial was erected in that field, citing the courageous actions of those passengers on United Airlines Flight 93, who undoubtedly saved the lives of countless others, had the plane reached its intended target.

Satan is a terrorist by nature. As defined by the Oxford English Dictionary, a terrorist is a "person who uses unlawful violence and intimidation, especially against civilians, in the pursuit of political aims."[21] In the same vein, our enemy goes against God's laws by coercive means, against the citizens of heaven in pursuit of his own personal gain. He accomplishes this by attempting to invade and hijack our consciences. To hijack is to "unlawfully seize or take over something and force it to go to a different destination or use it for one's own purposes."[22]

Obviously, Satan uses devious means to convince our consciences that God's ways and what biblical standards have to say aren't absolute truth. Recall his power of persuasion with Eve in the garden of Eden:

> He [the serpent] said to the woman, "Did God *really* say, 'You must not eat from *any* tree in the garden?'" The woman said to the serpent, "We may eat fruit from the trees in the garden, but God did say, 'You must not eat fruit from the tree that is in the middle of the garden, and you must not touch it, or you will die.'" "You will *not* certainly die," the serpent said to the woman. "For God knows that when you eat from it your eyes will be opened, and you will be like God, knowing good and evil." (Genesis 3:1–4, emphasis added)

We can see that the serpent began his assault on Eve's conscience by playing dumb and twisting God's command from *you must not eat from the tree in the middle of the garden* to you must not eat of *any* tree. Eve, in turn, corrects the serpent's "error," but not only that, she adds to God's directive of not *eating* from the tree by telling the serpent they were forbidden from *touching* it as well. The serpent, realizing that his subtle challenge was starting to work its poison, assuages Eve's conscience into believing that she and Adam would not surely die and that God possibly had unworthy motives (i.e., not wanting his creations to become like him or to be morally independent of him). Once Adam and Eve's eyes were open to the truth, they realized that their consciences had been turned against them—that the so-called "snake in the grass" had sidetracked their idyllic existence toward a mortal future.

When Satan tries to hijack our consciences, he uses many of the same tactics that he used with Adam and Eve. Often, he subtly weaves his lies and half-truths into our inner being, starting with low-level guilt and gradually expanding our acceptance and our justification of our actions. Consider the following real-life statements that many people (including Christians) have made:

- There's nothing wrong with going 10 miles over the speed limit, especially if no one else is on the road (guilty!).
- Who's going to miss a box of paper clips, ream of paper, etc.? This company has so much overhead.
- If it's not reported to the IRS, then it doesn't make sense for me to report that extra income from my craft show.
- Whoops, the waitress forgot to add those drinks to the check. Oh well, that's on her.
- Man, I can't believe I sideswiped that car in the parking lot. But there are already plenty of dings and scratches. What's one more scrape on an old heap?
- I'm pretty much done with my work, so I might as well catch up with Facebook until it's time to leave the office.

The Tempter knows where to attack, and he does so with a surgeon's precision. He often aims at nominal infractions that produce the lowest levels of guilt, convincing his victims that in the whole scheme of immoral actions, ours are negligible if not outright permissible. As these marginal types of sins begin to accumulate and take hold, we are more inclined to venture up the scale of rationalization (remember *rational lies*?). Desensitization gradually sets in, lulling us into a state of complacency and leaving us with a conscience that is numb to both shame and guilt. This is why the Apostle Paul reminds us to "take captive every thought to make it obedient to Christ" (2 Corinthians 10:5b). Why? As Paul mentions in verse 3, "Though we live in the world, we do not wage war as the world does. The weapons we fight with are not the weapons of the world. On the contrary, they have divine power to demolish strongholds. We demolish arguments and every pretension that sets itself up against the knowledge of God."

Dressed for Battle—Part One

Paul was concerned that those under his charge would be led astray just as Eve had (2 Corinthians 11:3). He knew the power of the Enemy's lies, and for this reason, he encouraged his readers to dwell on "whatever is true, whatever is noble, whatever is right, whatever is pure, whatever is lovely, whatever is admirable—if anything is excellent or praiseworthy—think about such things" (Philippians 4:8). When you are wearing the breastplate of righteousness, along with your belt of truth, your mind is filled with "right" thinking. In turn, you are protected and insulated from Satan's attacks. Just as the passengers on Flight 93 attempted to reclaim the aircraft from the terrorist hijackers, we too must make every attempt to regain and maintain control of our thought life and ultimately rescue our consciences from Satan's subtle sway.

> Arise, soldiers of Christ, throw away the works of darkness and put on the armor of light. (Saint Cecilia)

*The whole concept of distorted thinking has also influenced the field of psychotherapy, leading to the emergence of various types of treatment known as cognitive-behavioral therapy. Fundamentally, cognitive-based therapies acknowledge that patterns of negative thinking can often lead to negative feelings and attributions, often resulting in mental health disorders such as anxiety, fear, and depression. Based largely on the work of Dr. Aaron Beck, the goal of cognitive therapy is to challenge these negative thoughts (which are often irrational, exaggerated, or simply untrue) and to replace them with more positive or rational ways of thinking. Please refer to heritagecounselingcenter.blogspot.com/2015/03/disarming-cognitive-distortions-with.html to learn more about these cognitive distortions, along with their biblical counter-threads.[23]

Chapter 8:
Dressed for Battle— Part Two
(Outfitted Head to Toe)

The Shoes of Peace

There seems to be no limit as to the types of shoes available to a person, depending on the function or purpose for which they are to be used. There are dress shoes, casual shoes, athletic shoes (don't even get me started), work shoes, sandals, and boots. A ballet dancer wears a different shoe than a tap dancer. Tom Brady wears a different shoe than LeBron James. A construction worker wears different footwear than a nurse. You get the point.

The Roman soldier's shoes were designed for a particular purpose and function as well. Often they were made of bronze or brass and included two parts—the greave and the shoe itself. The greave was a tube-like piece of metal that ran from the top of the knee down past the lower leg and finally rested on the upper portion of foot. It was made to fit around the calf of a soldier's leg, protecting the leg from being seriously injured in battle.

The soldier's shoes were equipped on the bottom with extremely sharp spikes one to two inches long. John McArthur (quoted in

Kay Arthur's *Lord Is It Warfare?*) points out that "in the time of Roman wars, there was a common military practice (similar to the land mines of today) of planting sticks in the ground which had been sharpened to a razor-point, and concealing them so that they were almost invisible. This was a very effective tactic because, if the soldier's foot was pierced, he wouldn't be able to walk; and if he couldn't walk, he was totally debilitated."[1] As such, the soldier's footwear needed to be sturdy, protective, and durable against both natural and manmade elements.

So why, then, did Paul choose the Roman soldier's shoes to illustrate the idea of peace? "Peace," says Rick Renner, "is an awesome weapon, both offensive and defensive. Peace protects you but also provides a soldier with a brutal weapon to wield against the enemy."[2] Just as the shoe needed to be tied firmly to bottom of the feet to provide solid footing, we too must firmly tie peace around our lives or the affairs of life will easily knock our peace out of place.

"Peace [also] gives us a foundation so secure," Renner adds, "that we can step out in confident faith without being moved by what we see or what we hear."[3] In that sense, Renner offers two kinds of peace to consider. One is peace *with* God—that which a believer experiences when first coming to God for salvation. The second kind of peace—the peace *of* God—is a protective peace. It is the peace that passes understanding that holds Satan at bay, keeping him from employing his weapons of fear, anxiety, and worry that can easily choke the joys of the abundant life promised to all believers. "When the peace of God is ruling in your heart, mind, and emotions, you can forge your way through the rockiest of situations," says Renner. "Satan can't play games with your emotions or your mind when they are being governed by peace!"[4]

"Our peace shoes are go shoes," says Priscilla Shirer. "They are designed to move forward and announce the good news of victory. Powerful enough to tear down, demolish, and take back. They can go into the territory of your life that may currently be under enemy influence and get it back in Jesus' name."[5]

Dressed for Battle—Part Two

The Shield of Faith

I and about 95.5% of the male human race can probably agree that *Gladiator* is one of the greatest movies of all time (4.5% of you guys think *Captain America* is a better movie, but that's a discussion for another time). Both movies, however, involve a shield designed to protect the holder from bodily injury from the enemy's sword or other piercing weapons. In fact, Captain America's shield is his *only* weapon, and mostly a defensive one at that. His shield is made from a special indestructible alloy that is capable of absorbing kinetic energy and strong enough to absorb Hulk's brute strength and fend off an attack from Thor's mystical hammer.*

While the Roman soldier's shield carried none of the properties of Captain America's shield, it nonetheless served the purpose of protecting its bearer from bodily harm. As such, it needed to be made of strong and durable material to withstand numerous blows from the opposing force. Historical and archeological records suggest that while there were many types of Roman shields, the standard or typical shield carried into battle was fairly large—nearly the size of a small door (in fact, the Greek word for shield was *thureos* derived from *thura*, meaning "door"). Typically about two feet wide and four feet long, it was large enough to cover a soldier's body as he crouched down. Although it could be composed of various materials, often the shield was a large piece of wood covered by canvas and several layers of leather or animal skins drawn together tightly. Iron or metal could be embedded into the center of the shield and around its edges to give further protection and stability. Roman soldiers often rubbed their shields with oil to keep the leather supple and to avoid cracking over time.

When engaged in battler, Roman soldiers often faced the prospect of flaming arrows from the enemy. For this reason, they often soaked the shields in water beforehand to extinguish the flames. As a further military defensive strategy, small groups of Roman soldiers would close rank and huddle in with their shields facing out, thus forming a "turtle shell" that offered further protection.

Having a shield of faith means we are "acting like God is telling the truth," says Priscilla Shirer. Faith is the "process of adapting your behavior, your decisions, and ultimately, your whole lifestyle so that it accords with what God has asked you to do—without needing to see the evidence that it will all work out in the end . . . you choose to act in accordance with truth despite the fact that you can't see what the outcome will be. The act of faith is what becomes a shield of protection to guard against the enemy's attacks."[6]

Being a person of faith also means:

- Choosing to live with an unwavering confidence in God and his promises to you.
- Walking forward in accordance with truth as revealed in his Word and his personal directives for your life that align with it.
- By his power, pushing past the fear or doubts that may seek to paralyze you in insecurity, choosing instead to follow God where he is leading, trusting that he will take care of the rest.[7]

Having faith does not mean controlling God or making him abide by our wishes. Rather, it means gaining access to what God has already purposed to do for us. It's really less about us and more about God. Faith does not focus on the measure of our belief but on how "trustworthy, true, and loyal the object of that belief has proven Himself to be."[8] As Pastor Tony Evans has put it, "Faith is acting as if something is so even when it appears not to be so in order that it might be shown to be so simply because God said so."[9]

"If you are struggling to move forward in obedience to God," says Shirer, "you do not need bigger faith [but] need to realize how big your God is. The more faithful and strong you believe Him to be, the more willing you will be to depend on Him. Your level of faith will always be tied to your perception of God. If your perception of Him is faulty, your faith will be faulty. If your perception of Him is on point, your faith will be too. You don't need more faith; you need a more comprehensive and accurate view of the faithfulness of your

Dressed for Battle—Part Two

God."[10] As one pastor I know used to say, we don't need great faith in God, but faith in a great God. That's what Jesus was referring to when he said we only needed the faith of a mustard seed (Matthew 17:20).**

So how does one strengthen one's faith? Just as Roman soldiers soaked their shields in water prior to battle to extinguish the enemy's flaming arrows, so we should "soak" our faith in God's Word. Saturating our faith in scripture means we are well-prepared to handle any attack, lie, or accusation Satan sends our way. We are reminded in the book of Hebrews that God's Word is "alive and active. Sharper than any double-edged sword, it penetrates even to dividing soul and spirit, joints and marrow; it judges the thoughts and attitudes of the heart" (Hebrews 4:12). Moreover, we know that "all Scripture is God-breathed and is useful for teaching, rebuking, correcting and training in righteousness" (2 Timothy 3:16). Given these promises, how can we not be immersed in reading and studying God's Word? To not do so would be akin to going to war with a cardboard shield. Yet many Christians attempt to go through life in such fashion, without the Word of God getting into their minds and hearts to inform and guide their decisions and actions when under spiritual attack.

Likewise, our faith has been saturated—has been cleansed—with Christ's redeeming blood on the cross. "Since we have confidence to enter the Most Holy Place by the blood of Jesus, . . . let us draw near to God with a sincere heart and with the full assurance that faith brings, having our hearts sprinkled to cleanse us from a guilty conscience and having our bodies washed with pure water" (Hebrews 10:19, 22). As we go into battle, we have the full assurance through Christ's sacrificial blood that our sins have been forgiven and a guarantee of protection from the evil one.

Additionally, just as Roman soldiers used the "turtle maneuver" to form a protective barricade against the enemy, so we need the fellowship and camaraderie of other believers as a guard against our enemy. The expression "strength in numbers" could not be more relevant than to the Christian faith as God made us for community.

It is in community that we find our faith challenged, strengthened, and formed to withstand Satan's assaults. Just as a lion waits for its prey to wander away and stand apart from the herd, the devil latches on to those who are not strongly connected to a body of believers.

The Helmet of Salvation

The Roman helmet was obviously an important defensive piece of armor, designed to protect the soldier's head from blows from battleaxes, swords, and the like. The helmet also included metal pieces that shielded the sides of the face and jaws. Out of necessity, the helmet was made of heavy durable metal, designed to ward off a blow to the head.

The Roman helmet was also very ornate, often inscribed with decorative engravings and pictures. On the top of the helmet, many soldiers' helmets were adorned with a tall plume or brightly colored feather or horsehair. This was to give the soldier the appearance of being taller. Similarly, our salvation could be considered our "most gorgeous, most intricate, most elaborate, and most ornate gift God ever gave you. When someone is confident of his salvation and walking in that powerful reality, that person is noticeable!"[11]

Paul undoubtedly chose the helmet to represent our salvation in that our freedom in Christ—the result of his ultimate sacrifice for humankind—protects us from the penalty of sin and from the enemy's attacks on our faith. As Rick Renner points out, "If you don't walk in your salvation and all it entails, you may feel the brunt of the enemy's battleaxe coming to attack your mind and steal your victory. To face the adversary without your helmet of salvation is the equivalent of spiritual suicide."[12]

Much has been said in recent years about the NFL's policies for concussion-related injuries. As the medical histories of former pro football players have come to light, it has become quite apparent that relentless blows to the head during play have resulted in repeated concussions (sustained repetitive brain trauma), leading over time to degenerative brain disease known as chronic traumatic encephalopathy or CTE. While the NFL refused to acknowledge this research at first, it has since come to establish better protocols to ensure the safety of players who are concussed during a game. In addition, the design of football helmets have since come under greater scrutiny to afford better protection against head injuries—not just at the pro level, but also extending down to college, high school, and younger players.

Similarly, the Roman helmet, by protecting the head, also guarded the soldier's brain—the most important vital organ along with the heart. A soldier needed to think on his feet and could not afford to be mentally impaired by an unexpected blow to the head. Without his mental faculties intact, the Roman soldier would be of little use in defending himself or his comrades. If his shield and sword were unable to thwart his foe's attacks, then the Roman soldier needed to have a sturdy helmet as a backup measure.

"Carefully guard your thoughts [mind] because they are the source of true life," the author of Proverbs reminds us (Proverbs 4:23, CEV). How do we do this? It bears repeating, but for starters, we need to capture what enters our minds and ruthlessly examine it in the light of God's Word (2 Corinthians 10:5b). This implies that we can tame or recalibrate our thoughts to align them with what scripture says. As The Message translation puts it, we can fit "every loose thought and emotion and impulse into the structure of life shaped by Christ."

The Amazing Brain

Neuroscientists have used the term *neuroplasticity* to describe the brain's ability to reorganize itself with new neural connections. This is what happens when we apply Paul's principle of taking our thoughts captive. "When we take our thoughts captive, we are quite literally renewing and restoring our minds from a state of unhealthiness and deterioration to a state of wholeness and strength in God," writes Priscilla Shirer. "Tapping into our spiritual benefits package not only keeps us from falling prey to the enemy's deception, but also restores previous damage that's been done. When we apply our spiritual inheritance diligently and proactively, we literally change our minds—renewing and rewiring them through God's Word."[13]

Taking every thought captive is often easier said than done, but realigning our thinking is critical to our survival and witness in a fallen world. Truth be told, if you don't take your thoughts captive, your thoughts will take you captive. It also may take a lifetime to fully transform our thoughts into God's thoughts. Rick Warren offers the following acrostic (THINK) to help maintain our focus on this lifelong process:

> T—Test every thought, asking God to search and examine every thought. Don't believe everything you think.
>
> H—Helmet your head with salvation, which guarantees protection from Satan's fiery darts.
>
> I—Imagine great thoughts. Think and meditate on the great promises of God.
>
> N—Nourish a godly mind. Growth in godly thinking is not an option. We must study, reflect, meditate, and set our minds on things above.
>
> K—Keep on learning. If this is happening, then others should notice the progress in your life in your words and actions.[14]

More Than an Insurance Policy

Priscilla Shirer reminds that our salvation is more than "fire insurance"—more than a free ticket to paradise. Yes, we initially *receive* salvation when we first come to Christ in confession and belief, but we must also *apply* our salvation on a daily basis. The former redeems us, but the latter restores, protects, and shields us from Satan's daily assaults. "Salvation," Shirer adds, "is not just a past-tense event (known as justification or being made righteous in the eyes of God) with future-tense implications. As we live underneath its blessing, we enjoy a vibrant, living, daily reality in the present (known as sanctification or being made or becoming holy)."[15]

Our intellectual understanding and comprehension of salvation and all that it encompasses must be ingrained in our minds. When our minds are convinced of these realities—when our minds are trained and taught to think correctly in terms of our salvation—that knowledge becomes a protective helmet in our lives! When you walk in your helmet of salvation, you think like God thinks, you reason like God reasons, you believe like God believes, and you act like God acts.[16]

I have an acquaintance who rides a motorcycle but who refuses to wear a helmet. When confronted about this, he would simply reply, "Well, everyone has to go sometime." To me, this spoke of a naïve, short-sighted view of life. Not wearing a helmet essentially revealed that this person's life perspective was not based on anything secure or sure but fleeting. By comparison, the helmet of salvation represents our inheritance in Christ. Choosing not to wear it means leaving our mind exposed, unprotected, like bikers who don't wear a helmet but instead, take their chances on the road. Conversely, as Christians, we have no excuse to not wear God's helmet of salvation. The price for this helmet has been paid in full by Christ. As such, we should wear it daily and with the conviction that Jesus paid it all, allowing us to go to battle as immortal warriors.

The Sword of the Spirit

The sword is the only offensive weapon Paul lists under the armor of God, but as they say, the best defense is a good offense. While many types of swords were used by Roman soldiers, Paul was most likely referring to one type—*machiara* in the Greek. This weapon was approximately 19 inches long, and both sides of the blade were honed to razor sharpness. The Greek word *distomos*—meaning "two-mouthed"—also refers to a two-sided sword that was more deadly in warfare as it could easily cut two ways. In a spiritual sense, one edge might constitute the Word of God that initially proceeded from the mouth of God, while the second edge might refer to the Word of

God as it proceeds from our own mouths. The tip of this sword also turned inward to inflict the most damage to the enemy (intending to not just kill, but also to literally rip or shred the opponent's innards). Similarly, God's sword of the Spirit has the potential to rip our enemy to shreds when used appropriately.

Rick Renner refers to a *rhema*, a "specific word or message that the Holy Spirit quickens in our hearts and minds at a specific time and for a special purpose."[17] Many of us have had the experience of recalling a particular scripture or of having a passage come to mind in the midst of a trying situation. In those moments, it is likely God's Spirit is activating a rhema word that provides us with the action, guidance, or knowledge to address the situation we are in. As Renner points out, it is not necessary to memorize large sections of scripture to have the sword of the Spirit at your ready. But when you respond in faith to that "freshly given, freshly spoken rhema word from the Holy Spirit, it will act like a mighty blade in your hand, releasing a mighty force of divine power that is capable of destroying the work of the devil in your life."[18]

When Jesus was severely tempted in the desert, he wielded the rhema Word of God like a mighty blade. Jesus had to know the Word of God completely; otherwise, he would have been deceived by Satan's deceptive ploy (because Satan knows the Bible). Be ready for your own testing in the wilderness, because when you begin to take new territory for the Kingdom of God, the devil will try to stop you. As soon as you begin to grow in your knowledge of God's Word and make spiritual progress, Satan will try to slow you down. The enemy doesn't want you to make any progress in your spiritual life.[19]

As a child, I remember watching Disney's version of *The Sword and the Stone*, a retelling of the story of King Arthur's coming into his kingdom. A sword had been securely placed into a rock by Merlin the wizard, with the stipulation that the one who could pull the sword from the stone was worthy to be named the king of the land. In much the same way, Jesus was able to raise the sword of the Spirit on our behalf and through his salvific act, we can lay claim to the same power and authority Jesus had in his ministry and his resurrection (Romans 8:11), including the power to "demolish arguments and every pretension that sets itself up against the knowledge of God, [taking] captive every thought to make it obedient to Christ" (2 Corinthians 10:5)—even to do greater things than Jesus did (John 14:12). We need only call on the Holy Spirit to activate this power in Jesus' name—power that is promised and available to all believers.

The Lance of Prayer and Supplication

Paul was quite thorough in describing the various pieces of a Roman soldier's armor from head to toe. However, he omitted one important piece of the soldier's arsenal—the spear or lance. Whether or not this was an oversight or intentional on Paul's part, we know he did refer to "putting on the *whole* armor of God," implying a full set of weaponry. In Ephesians 6:18, Paul ends his instruction on spiritual armor with the directive to "pray in the Spirit on all occasions with all kinds of prayers and requests." Rick Renner refers to this as the lance of prayer and supplication.[20]

In ancient warfare, lances and spears were used for a variety of purposes in battle, and so they came in different sizes and shapes. Most spears were intended to be thrown with great force from a distance and with accuracy so as to incapacitate the enemy. When thrown in an upward motion in a high arc, a spear could take a foe completely by surprise as they would not see the long narrow missile until it was directly upon him. Lances by function were used more in a thrusting motion from the ground or from horseback so as to keep the adversary out of striking distance while also disabling him. Again, different weapons with different functions.

Similarly, our prayers can be thrust like spears into the spiritual realm to disarm Satan. When hurled with great intention and in the power of the Spirit, prayer—especially the collective prayers of all the saints—can present an impenetrable defense in the face of evil. Likewise, our prayer *arsenal* can take different forms as well. We have many types of prayer at our disposal, including prayers of supplication, petition, intercession, and thanksgiving, to name a few. No one type of prayer is better than the others; we simply need to employ the lance of prayer when needed. And Paul makes no distinction as to when to pray except to do so *on all occasions*. His implication here is that there is no situation or circumstance that is not worthy of being lifted in prayer. We are also to pray *in the Spirit* since "we do not know what we ought to pray for, but the Spirit himself intercedes for us through wordless groans" (Romans 8:26). Lastly, we are to remain alert, like prepared soldiers, and stand in defense of our fellow warriors at all times by praying for all of them.

In the movie *War Room*, an elderly woman has a special closet she has dedicated to praying, calling it her "War Room" because as she puts it, "In order to stand up and fight the enemy, you need to get on your knees and pray." In military lingo, a war room refers to the headquarters or command central where many of the decisions about battle planning takes place. While we don't need to be so tactical as to have an actual prayer room or closet, we can become more strategic in our prayer lives by making it a priority, by using different types of prayers, and by interceding for others in our prayers. "But when you pray, go into your room [or closet], close the door and pray to your Father, who is unseen," said Jesus. "[And] *then* your Father, who sees what is done in secret, will reward you" (Matthew 6:6). Additionally, as we prepare for battle on our knees, God has promised to hear us and respond in kind:

> If my people, who are called by my name, will humble themselves and pray and seek my face and turn from their wicked ways, then I will hear from heaven, and I will forgive their sin and will heal their land. (2 Chronicles 7:14)

> The Lord is far from the wicked, but he hears the prayer of the righteous. (Proverbs 15:29)

> Therefore I tell you, whatever you ask for in prayer, believe that you have received it, and it will be yours. (Mark 11:24)

> Do not be anxious about anything, but in every situation, by prayer and petition, with thanksgiving, present your requests to God. And the peace of God, which transcends

all understanding, will guard your hearts and your minds in Christ Jesus. (Philippians 4:6–7)

This is the confidence we have in approaching God: that if we ask anything according to his will, he hears us. (1 John 5:14)

Is anyone among you sick? Let them call the elders of the church to pray over them and anoint them with oil in the name of the Lord. And the prayer offered in faith will make the sick person well; the Lord will raise them up. If they have sinned, they will be forgiven. (James 5:14–15)

Onward Christian Soldier

So, having received your marching orders, are you prepared to follow Christ into battle? If so, it is vital that you count the costs, because the dangers and ramifications are real.

> Yet in saying, "Count the cost," what am I saying? Am I suggesting that it is possible to live as a Christian without warfare? For this is not true. The real counting should have been done before you became a Christian. *To acknowledge Jesus as Savior and Lord is to join an army. Whether you know it or not, you have enlisted.* The only other options open to you is to become a deserter, to hide your uniform and pretend you are someone whom you are not. Now to be a deserter is not to *leave* the army (celestial regulations make no provision for the discharge of personnel) but to evade your responsibility to your commanding officer.[22]

Ultimately, our choice involves either fighting or fleeing, loyalty or desertion. If any indecision or doubt exists between obeying Christ and legitimate but idolatrous objects of our desires, Christ must always come first. Only by adopting the attitude of a soldier and by obeying orders without concern of the consequences are our fears allayed and our peace restored. Yes, war is taxing and inevitably involves suffering, but "take your share of suffering," Paul writes to Timothy, "as a good soldier of Christ Jesus" (2 Timothy 2:3).

Today, how many of us "play the game" of Christianity vs. engage in "hand-to-hand combat" with the enemy? Instead of arming ourselves with the belt of truth, the breastplate of righteousness, and feet fitted with the Gospel, are we more concerned with being Christian-ly fashionable (i.e., T-shirts emblazoned with "I'm in the Lord's Army" or "Jesus is my Commander in Chief")? How well will our bumper stickers and fish magnets protect us from Satan's "flaming arrows"? Do we truly claim a certain and firm hope (helmet) of our ultimate salvation or continue to live in fear and skepticism? And do our "swords" (God's Word revealed through his Spirit) stand sharpened and ready for battle, or do they sit idly aside, tarnished and dull from disuse?

The enemy wants you to think that life is a playground, not a battleground. As soldiers—as warriors—under God's command, we are not to shirk our duties nor slumber at our watches, "but in your hearts revere Christ as Lord. Always be prepared to give an answer to everyone who asks you to give the reason for the hope that you have" (1 Peter 3:15), like "experienced soldiers prepared for battle with every type of weapon . . . with undivided loyalty" (1 Chronicles 12:33) and "prepared in season and out of season" (2 Timothy 4:2).

Armor Check

In his book *The Checklist Manifesto*, Dr. Atul Gawande explores the highly effective use of a very simple tool—the checklist—to ensure integrity and compliance in meeting goals and avoiding human error and distraction.[23] Because human memory is fallible and because being human, we often tend to skip over important steps, checklists can serve as an important safeguard. So employing this simple but effective technique, let's take personal inventory of our spiritual armor:***

Dressed for Battle—Part Two

- ☐ The Belt of Truth
  - How well are you strengthening and protecting your spiritual core?
  - How often do you regularly engage in Bible reading, study, and meditation?
  - If the truth of God's Word is not central to your life, what is? What do you need to replace with God's Word?
  - What evidence is there that you are bearing fruit and multiplying?
  - Do you daily reference your thoughts, actions, and worldview with the truth of God's word?
  - Do you synchronize your convictions with God's character and purposes?
- ☐ The Breastplate of Righteousness
  - Are you daily claiming the righteousness God has credited to you?
  - Are you growing in righteousness through holy habits (Bible study, prayer, fasting, etc.)?
  - How are you guarding against distorted thinking (attacks of the mind)?
  - Do you have your sights set on godly pursuits, or are they directed toward temporal, short-sighted interests (attacks of the will)?
  - Are you allowing runaway emotions to determine your decisions (attacks of the emotions)?
  - Are you cultivating healthy spiritual scruples (defending against attacks of the conscience)?

CLOTHED with CHRIST

- ☐ The Shoes of Peace
  - Are you allowing the peace of God to cover you and keep Satan at bay?
  - Are you daily claiming Christ's victory over sin and death that leads to peace?
  - Are you living at peace with your decisions, your relationships, and your lifestyle?
- ☐ The Shield of Faith
  - Is your faith based on a great God and his promises?
  - What does your level of faith say about your perception of God?
  - Are you aligning your life with God's commands and purposes, believing his ways are right and true?
  - How well do you push past fears, doubts, and insecurities—putting full trust in God and his ways?
  - Are you "soaking" your faith daily in God's Word?
  - Are you strengthening your faith by staying linked to a community of believers?
- ☐ The Helmet of Salvation
  - Having received your salvation, how well are you applying it on a daily basis?
  - How are you tangibly working out your salvation? (Philippians 2:12–13)
  - Do your thoughts, decisions, beliefs, and actions mirror God's and Christ's?
  - Your salvation is secure—are you living like it?
  - Are you guarding your mind from toxic thoughts or errant patterns?

Dressed for Battle—Part Two

- How are you renewing/rewiring your mind through God's Word?

☐ The Sword of the Spirit

- How are you growing in your knowledge of God's Word?
- Are you committing scripture to memory?
- Are you sharpening swords with other believer through communal study?
- Are you praying for and seeking God's *rhema* word from his Spirit?

☐ The Lance of Prayer and Supplication

- Do you have a regular prayer life? Are you faithful in praying for others?
- How do you pray? You might consider the following acronym as a model:

A—Adoration (giving praise to God)

C—Confession (asking God to forgive your sins)

T—Thanksgiving (thanking God for his blessings)

S—Supplication (asking God to intervene on the behalf of myself and others)

"Actionable intel" is a military term referring to information that has been gathered about an opposing force that can be used against it in future battles. In a spiritual context, says Priscilla Shirer, we are given actionable intel from what God has revealed to us through his Holy Spirit—information that we can use to craft a strategy to employ against our enemy Satan to gain victory over sin.[23] After reviewing your responses to the above checklist, develop an action plan for the coming week, focusing on one particular piece of armor. Continue to review this checklist periodically and modify your actionable intel as needed to address any chinks in your armor.

CLOTHED with CHRIST

As further evidence of your commitment to put on God's armor, consider praying the following prayer based on Ephesians 6:10–18:

Equip me, Lord:

- **With the belt of truth** (v. 14). May your truth rule in my heart and be in my mind and on my lips today.

- **With the breastplate of righteousness** (v. 14). Apart from you there is no righteousness, but through Jesus I have been "born again" and have been made righteous in your sight. May I live as a righteous person.

- **With feet fitted with the readiness that comes from the Gospel of peace** (v. 15). May I reflect the Gospel in my words and actions, that through me, with my every encounter, others may be drawn one step closer to you.

- **With the shield of faith** (v.16). May I take you at your Word concerning promises about the present and future—promises of everlasting love, abundant life, and so much more.

- **With the helmet of salvation** (v. 17). Remind me that nothing can separate me from your love and that I've been saved by grace. In your grace, help me to say "no" to all ungodliness and worldly passions and to live a self-controlled, upright, and godly life (Titus 2:12–13).

- **And with the sword of the Spirit, the Word of God** (v. 17). May your Holy Spirit reign in my life and bring to my mind just the right Bible verses to be in my heart and on my lips. May I be "filled with the Spirit" and ready with Scripture as you were, Jesus, when the devil tempted you.

- **Finally, keep me in an attitude of prayer** (v. 18). Remind me to "pray in the Spirit on all occasions." Cause me to be alert and always praying for the saints; to be joyful and to give thanks in everything (see 1 Thessalonians 5:16–18).[24]

Dressed for Battle—Part Two

> Put on all the armor of the Lord. Not just the pretty stuff.
> (Mark Vonnegut)

*For the uninitiated, Hulk is a fictional comic book superhero who is a green-skinned, uber-muscular and strong humanoid whose alter-ego is scientist Bruce Banner. Thor is also a superhero based on a Nordic deity who possesses an enchanted hammer that allows him to fly and perform other superhuman feats.

**A mustard seed is only 1 to 2 millimeters in diameter, but depending on the variety, the tree can grow 6 to 20 feet tall.

***While a checklist can be used as an effective tool to monitor spiritual growth, caution should be taken to avoid their legalistic application. We obviously want to shun anything that smacks of works-oriented, performance-based actions. Rather, consider this less a checklist than a spiritual "checkup" of how you are responding to God's grace and Jesus' ultimate sacrifice.

Chapter 9:
In Your Glad Rags
(Dressed for the Homecoming)

> Heaven will be the perfection we've always longed for. All the things that made Earth unlovely and tragic will be absent in heaven. (Billy Graham)

> The day of one's birth is a good day for the believer, but the day of death is the greatest day that a Christian can ever experience in this world because that is the day he goes home, the day he walks across the threshold, the day he enters the Father's house. (R. C. Sproul)

Up until now, we've discussed the various aspects of being clothed with Christ. Up from muck and mire, God formed humans in his image—physically unclothed but without shame. With the fall of Adam and Eve, guilt and shame ruled the day, requiring physical coverings to hide the evidence of their sin, symbolic of the barrier that divided humans from God and altering that divine relationship (while also signifying God's compassion for his children). To restore that relationship, God sent his son, Jesus, in human form as a ransom—as payment for the penalty of our sins. Through his act of grace, God restored us as his sons and daughters, clothing us in Christ's righteousness, love, and mercy by his Son's death and resurrection. Jesus' life and ministry showed his followers how they should live, adorned with love toward God and others. The Apostle Paul taught us how to live in this world, dressed for the battle between heavenly and evil forces while putting off our old natures, like old, worn-out clothes. He cautioned against lukewarm or carnal Christians wearing sheep's (deceptive) clothing and encouraged us to adapt our "style" when sharing our faith with nonbelievers. In retrospect, God has clothed his children—those who believe and follow Christ—with his very presence by the Holy Spirit. On our end, we must intentionally live our lives accordingly, choosing daily to "put on" the fruits of the Spirit and emulating Jesus' qualities and life.

The Great Beyond

If we've confessed faith in Jesus and attempted to live as "clothed with Christ," then God has promised that we would someday reside with him, in a place where there will be no more death or mourning or crying or pain (Revelation 21:4). Jesus, too, told his disciples that he was going to prepare a place for them. When he told them that he was leaving them, it was to make ready his eventual return as Bridegroom to retrieve his Bride—the Church.

In Paul's second letter to the church in Corinth, he speaks of that day when Christ returns and our earthly bodies will be destroyed and replaced with eternal ones:

> For we know that if the earthly tent we live in is destroyed, we have a building from God, an eternal house in heaven, not built by human hands. Meanwhile we groan, longing to be clothed with our heavenly dwelling, because when we are clothed, we will not be found naked. For while we are in this tent, we groan and are burdened, because we do not wish to be unclothed but to be clothed with our heavenly dwelling so that what is mortal may be swallowed up by life. (2 Corinthians 5:1–4)

Paul's reference to an "earthly tent" was consistent with some ancient writings that compared being clothed to being inside a house—both

In Your Glad Rags

being external and offering some degree of protection. In fact, the term for a garment worn by the poorer class is derived from a word meaning "little house." It is likely that Paul was using the images of an earthly tent and heavenly dwelling to draw contrasts between the temporal and the eternal, between nakedness and being clothed, between mortality and life unending.

If you have ever gone camping (I mean *real* camping in a tent), you know that tents offer some amount of protection from the elements—from wind, rain, and those pesky mosquitoes. As a young boy when camping with my dad or with my scout troop, we did not have the luxury of a nice, zippered-in nylon tent with an actual floor. Instead, we used canvas tents with no floor, no zippers, and no ventilation. These were no doubt comparable, if not identical, to the army-issued tents of World War II (I kid you not!). They offered no real protection from anything—creeping, slithering creatures found their way beneath the bottom of the tent walls, rain pelted the tent roof only to eventually soak through and rain *inside* the tent, summer heat created suffocating spa-like conditions, and seasonal chilly temperatures penetrated the various gaps in the canvas to numb any exposed digits and facial appendages. My one scouting experience with winter Polar Bear Camp was everything it had espoused to be—it was truly intended for polar bears, not humans.

Besides the musty smell of old canvas, my memories of camping included some amount of moaning and groaning because of those times when conditions were less than favorable. I imagine the Israelites, too, had their share of kvetching, spending forty years wandering in the wilderness, continually tearing down and pitching their mobile dwellings. The condition of these tents, I suspect, deteriorated greatly over time, requiring the owners to repeatedly mend and patch the cloth or animal skins after exposure to the elements. How great must have been the nomads' joy when they finally reached their promised destination and were able to build permanent homes.

Camping, for most of us, is meant to be a temporary experience, and while it may bring moments of great enjoyment, it is always good to return home and sleep in one's own bed surrounded by four secure walls and a roof over one's head. Similarly, our time *camped out* here on earth is meant to be a momentary period until we enter our permanent, *eternal* home. As our physical bodies begin to age and deteriorate, we literally groan from the aches and pains. Our spiritual selves, too, groan from the discomforts of this broken world, longing for the day when we will be made completely whole. And this day, as Jesus promised, will eventually come.

Dressed to the Nines

For believers, it's difficult to imagine this side of heaven what form our spiritual bodies will assume. I think we can pretty well dispel with the notion of sprouting wings and playing harps (who came up with that image?). Personally, I hope that my guise will bear some resemblance to a chiseled Adonis (although that would be selfish on my part). Perhaps we'll all bear the likeness of a kindly, middle-aged man wearing a cardigan sweater and laced-up sneakers (you know Mr. Rogers' neighborhood has to have taken up some real estate in heaven, right?).

The only inkling we get of our appearance-to-be comes from the book of Revelation. Several times John of Patmos, recalling his visions of heaven, refers to God's people as dressed in white (3:4–5, 4:17–18) or wearing white robes (6:10–11, 7:9–10). The significance of the color white is that it often denotes "purity" or "righteousness." It could also signify something that is unblemished, holy, or blameless. Think of a bride's white wedding dress, symbolizing virginity and innocence. Or a clean, spotless blanket of newly fallen snow. Or Ivory soap—although it's supposedly only $99^{44}/_{100}$% pure (Hmm, I wonder what that other .56% consists of?). At any rate, white robes or not, we will finally appear before our God and Creator as pure, spotless beings—transformed into that state of holy perfection we had strived to attain while still outfitted in our earthly bodies.

If you've ever attended a formal ball, cotillion, or black-tie affair (okay, me neither), you know that people tend to dress up pretty

In Your Glad Rags

fancy-like. Tuxedos and full-length gowns are the proper attire of the hour—no exceptions. Attendees are *dressed to the nines*, so to speak, and anyone attired otherwise is barred from attending.*

Jesus spoke of this in his parable of the marriage banquet (Matthew 22:1–14). In short, a king prepared a wedding banquet for his son. He invited members of the A-list of the day who outright refused to attend or rejected his invitation for any number of reasons. The king then decided to invite whoever he could get, sending his servants out into the streets and surrounding neighborhood to welcome others to the banquet—rich and poor, good and bad alike. All who were invited were provided with proper wedding attire so that when they entered the banquet, they looked as if they belonged—as if they were part of the royal party. One guest, however, was not dressed in the appropriate attire and was subsequently banished from the banquet.

This parable paints a picture of God's invitation to enter his kingdom—first to his chosen people (the Jews) and then to gentiles (non-Jews) when the first-order guests rejected the invitation. As for the guest who is dressed improperly for the banquet, the case could be made that for those invited to the banquet, not all will be dressed in Christ's robe of righteousness. In a sense, this guest represents professed Christians who choose to wear their own righteousness instead of Christ's.[1]

These many references to being dressed in white or in wedding clothes, or to our bodies undergoing a significant transformation upon Christ's return, signify a moral and spiritual completeness—the final realization of spiritual perfection, if you will. The process of a believer's sanctification will finally realize its conclusion as we assume the full and exact embodiment of our risen and triumphant King. Literal or symbolic, our bodies will take on a different form in the new paradise in line with our Maker's image and character. *Then we will be like him,* the Apostle Paul reminds us (1 John 3:2), *for we shall see him as he is.*

Paul also reminds us of this transformation in his first letter to the Corinthian church:

> I declare to you, brothers and sisters, that flesh and blood cannot inherit the kingdom of God, nor does the perishable inherit the imperishable. Listen, I tell you a mystery: We will not all sleep, but we will all be changed—in a flash, in the twinkling of an eye, at the last trumpet. For the trumpet will sound, the dead will be raised imperishable, and we will be changed. For the perishable must clothe itself with the imperishable, and the mortal with immortality. When the perishable has been clothed with the imperishable, and the mortal with immortality, then the saying that is written will come true: "Death has been swallowed up in victory." (1 Corinthians 5:50–54)

Taken in this sense,

> Being clothed in Christ doesn't mean only to bear the moral image of Jesus, to reflect His character, and to live out the principles that He taught us. In other words, it's not just a legal change, not just a moral change: it also will include a radical *physical* change. Our mortal flesh, our aching and hurting and dying flesh, will be clothed with the same kind of immortal body that the resurrected Jesus had. Talk about a change of clothing, talk about wearing a new garment! That's the ultimate hope that awaits us, the only hope that really makes our faith worthwhile.[2]

Rags to Riches

The Gospel proclaims the redemptive story of Jesus paying the price for our salvation as an outflow of God's grace. Much like the tale of the father welcoming home his prodigal son (Luke 15:11–32), God takes us in our filthy rags and places his majestic robe around us. God's story of grace is about getting rid of our sackcloths of sadness and despair and clothing ourselves in coverings of forgiveness and joy. It's about changing our status from *homeless* to *homebound*. From orphaned to adopted, lost to found, poor to rich. It's a true "rags to riches" story.

In Your Glad Rags

Halie was a young black woman who grew up in a poor section of New Orleans in the early 1900s, residing in a three-room dwelling that housed thirteen people. Raised by her aunt after her mother died, Halie faced significant financial hardships that forced her to quit school in the fourth grade and begin working at home. She soon discovered a talent for singing at a young age, beginning with her involvement in her church's choir. In later years, her pure, soulful voice was noticed by others in the field of gospel music. In 1937 she made her first gospel recordings, but it wasn't until 1948 when gospel music began to gain recognition that she recorded the song "Move On Up a Little Higher," which sold one million copies nationwide. Touring but battling segregation and racism along the way, Halie was eventually invited to perform at Carnegie Hall in 1950 for the First Negro Gospel Music Festival. In 1954, she recorded the first of thirty albums for Columbia Records. Later appearing on various variety shows and collaborating with the likes of Duke Ellington, Halie achieved great popularity and financial success that were met with severe racial backlash and even threats by white neighbors who protested her living in their Chicago suburb. Consequently, Halie became involved with the civil rights movement of the 1960s and eventually joined forces with Martin Luther King, Jr., singing "I've Been 'Buked" at the 1963 march in Washington, D.C, site of Dr. King's "I Have a Dream" speech. Halie also sang at President John F. Kennedy's inauguration and funeral and later at Martin Luther King's funeral. By 1972, after battling years of health problems, Halie passed away at the age of 60. Having conquered poverty, racism, and hardship, Halie—Mahalia Jackson—has become known as the greatest gospel singer of all time.[3]

Mahalia's journey from a poor, unschooled black girl to a gospel singing sensation is a remarkable account. She recognized at a young age the musical gift God had blessed her with and honored that gift by refusing to sing or record any secular music. But the true rags-to-riches story came the moment Mahalia passed from this world at age 60. Even though her physical body eventually failed her, as a believer in Jesus Christ, she was granted the promise of exchanging her mortal body for an immortal one. At her last breath, she experienced the miraculous transformation of becoming clothed with her heavenly "dwelling"—a new wardrobe fit for eternity.

Until Then?

We can have hope in what lies ahead, but in the meantime, what are we to do with the life we have been given? We can err in one of three ways. We can focus our thoughts on our future glory in heaven at the expense of neglecting our mission on earth ("being so heavenly minded that we are of no earthly good," goes the saying). Or we can devote our remaining time obsessing about how our earthly tent is fading away even though we're assured of a new body one day. Or we can engage in frivolous pursuits that ignore or neglect our commission to "go and make disciples of all nations" (i.e., playing the "church game" while ignoring Jesus' call to discipleship).

To avoid making any of these mistakes, we should assume a kingdom mentality. "A kingdom mentality includes the anticipation of heaven," says Pastor Brad Andres, "but its dual reality makes us focus on what we can do here and now to help grow God's kingdom."[4] As Christians we know that God's kingdom is not just a future reality but is right here and now. "Repent, for the kingdom of heaven is at hand," John the Baptist declared as he prepared his listeners for Jesus' coming. "The time is fulfilled, and the kingdom of God is at hand," proclaimed Jesus at the beginning of his ministry. And as he sent out his disciples for ministry, Jesus told them to announce, "The kingdom of heaven has come near." During the time of Jesus' life on earth, God's kingdom had arrived. Andres explains this "kingdom right now" mentality further:

> A kingdom mentality understands that the experience of eternal life starts the moment we accept Jesus as our Lord and Savior . . . [and] will also run on for all eternity. God's kingdom is a present reality, something that has been initiated on earth. However, the completion of His kingdom rule is still yet to be fully realized. . . . [In the meantime, we

are to be] living out our eternal life in the balance of heaven and earth.[5] [words in brackets added]

For many of us, especially those of us in our retirement years, we are content to sit back and enjoy the "down" time we have earned from working 40-plus years, raising a family, serving others, etc. However, nowhere in the Bible does it mention anything about retirement. In fact, the idea of retiring from work is a fairly "recent" notion, first emerging in the late 19th and early 20th centuries. Prior to this, most people worked until they died due to low life expectancies and lack of pension arrangements in those days.** Today, people are living longer than ever, with the average retiree expected to live another 20 to 30 years. So what to do with all that extra time?

For many retirees, lack of activity and purpose can lead to loneliness and even depression due to missing the social bonds they experienced at work. Sure, they may enjoy their newfound freedom and life of leisure for a time, but when asked about their overall happiness, the responses aren't always so rosy. Many report experiencing a "hole" in their lives that needs to be filled. So while the idea of a "never-ending vacation" sounds appealing on this side of retirement, another story can be told by many individuals who are in the midst of redefining their identity as retirees.

In Christian circles, the idea of retirement has come under strong scrutiny. Ralph Winter, founder of the U.S. Center for World Missions, was quoted as saying that "most men don't die of old age, they die of retirement."[6] Billy Graham, who passed away at the age of 99, claimed he would never retire. "I don't use that word because I'm not going to retire until God retires me," he said. "I don't find anybody in the Bible that retired. As long as there is a need for a proclamation of love and people need someone to turn to, I'm going to keep proclaiming the gospel."[7] Pastor and author John Piper is more forceful in his pronouncement against retirement:

> I tell you what a tragedy is. I'll read to you from *Reader's Digest* what a tragedy is: "Bob and Penny... took early retirement from their jobs in the Northeast five years ago

when he was 59 and she was 51. Now they live in Punta Gorda, Florida, where they cruise on their thirty-foot trawler, playing softball and collecting shells."

That's a tragedy. And people today are spending billions of dollars to persuade you to embrace that tragic dream. And I get forty minutes to plead with you: don't buy it. With all my heart I plead with you: don't buy that dream. The American Dream: a nice house, a nice car, a nice job, a nice family, a nice retirement, collecting shells as the last chapter before you stand before the Creator of the universe to give an account of what you did: "Here it is Lord — *my shell collection*! And I've got a nice swing, and look at my boat!"

Don't waste your life; don't waste it.[8]

Regardless your station in life, in what do you place your worth or security? What is displayed on your "trophy" shelf? Maybe your "value" doesn't come from seashells, but what about your golf handicap? Your Pinterest or Facebook posts? The number of books you've read or how many church committees you've served on? Is the focus on the number of steps on your Fitbit—the number of miles run—or the number of souls won? In what or in whom are you investing your remaining years in this life?

To reiterate, we may retire from a job or vocation, but we can never retire from our service to God as long as we still have life. Nowhere are we instructed in scripture that we are to enjoy our remaining time on earth or promised happiness (although it's true that God has blessed us with things to enjoy and receive pleasure from). However, we are not to neglect our commitment to serve and love God and others in our twilight years. If reading this serves as your wake-up call, you're welcome. If not, then consider the song, *Live Like You Were Dying* (made popular by singer Tim McGraw).[9] The lyrics portray a man who, while in his early forties, is given a cancer diagnosis and realizes he may not have much time left to live his life in full. But rather than crawling under a rock and waiting for death to overtake him, the man changes his perspective and decides to

In Your Glad Rags

live life to the fullest while there was still light in the day. He takes on experiences that he never took the time for before his diagnosis. More so, he becomes the person he needed to be in his relationships with God and others.

The essence of this song, I believe, is about taking risks and not squandering the time you have remaining on this earth. Chuck Swindoll once referred to a survey in which eighty-five-year-old people were asked what they regretted most about their lives. Their responses: Not spending more time reflecting in meditation and contemplation, not risking more, and not having done more things that would live on after their deaths.[10] I suppose many of us can relate to all of these responses, but having not risked more in life likely resonates with the majority of senior citizens (present company included). Excuses abound as to our reasons for not venturing out more in faith and to trust God and his Word, but uncertainty may be the chief justification for our lack of action. Satan tends to fill our minds with regretful *What if's* and *If onlys*, if only to reinforce our notions that we really don't have anything else to offer or contribute to God's kingdom here on earth. After all, doesn't it say in 1 Hesitations:

> For I know the plans I have for you, declares the Lord, plans for rest and recreation and not for toiling, to give you a nice retirement package and a vacation home.

Ah, no. Rather, in Jeremiah 29:11, God gives the prophet his word to the Jewish exiles living in Babylon. "'For I know the plans I have for you,' declares the LORD, 'plans to prosper you and not to harm you, plans to give you hope and a future.'" Since we, too, are exiles of a sort (remember, the earth is our temporary residence), we can claim these words as our own. Our future is both certain and secure, so that whatever we risk we pursue for God's kingdom will be blessed and honored. In God's economy, risk becomes investment, uncertainty is reframed as hope, and doubt is replaced by faith.

In his book *Half Time*, the late Bob Buford describes that important time of transition—of moving beyond the first half of the game of life into an opportunity to live the second half with new vision and purpose. He speaks specifically of finding your "One Thing"—that which leads to a state of joy and blessedness, something that you do so well that you would enjoy doing it without pay. Doing so may require releasing or relinquishing old patterns of doing things, your need to control, your fear of the unknown, and the idea of "deserved" time off. Finding your one thing also means that you may need to redefine what your life mission is and that you make learning a life-long process (especially studying subjects that apply to what is important to you and that relate to your life mission). Referencing Peter Drucker, Buford encourages individuals in the second half of life to consider what they have achieved (their competencies) and what they care deeply about (their passions) in forming their mid-life mission statement.[11]

I remember when I was about to turn the age of fifty (*has it really been that many years ago?*). It was a stark reminder that I had already lived just over half of my adult life and had reached a midlife milestone (not crisis, mind you). The ultimate decision before me was, *How should I now live? How should I live the remaining years I have left on this earth?* God impressed upon me that whether I had 10, 20, or 30-plus years left, I needed to live with intention and not waste the time for which I had been stewarded. If you are at a comparable stage in life, consider retirement as a brief period (maybe 3, 6, or 12 months) of "sabbatical rest to prepare the heart for a new season of fruitfulness," suggests Jeff Haanen, author of *An Uncommon Guide to Retirement: Finding God's Purpose for the Next Season of Life*.[12] Many Christian retirees are learning to reframe retirement as a "season of unique influence," he adds, where they are learning to release the power and control of the workplace and invest their wisdom in the lives of others. Instead of buying into the mindset that sees aging as a "problem to be solved . . . a new generation of older Americans see retirement as a contemporary social construct that affords them the opportunity to re-explore their God-given purpose for a new season of life . . . to serve God and neighbor as elders in their spheres of influence."[13]

In Your Glad Rags

As I write this, God has led me to continue my ministry to men in prison whose futures have been temporarily put on hold. I also serve as a mentor and life coach to young men whose futures lie just over the horizon. Whatever stage of life you may be in, God has ordained your life and time—start to finish—for his glory. And as you approach your twilight years, remember that you still have much to offer, if only but the wisdom from a life well-lived or from lessons learned from life's mistakes. Perhaps John Piper put it best:

> What will it mean to live those final years for the glory of Christ? How will we live them in such a way as to show that Christ is our highest Treasure? . . . Live dangerously for the one who loved you and died for you in his thirties. Don't throw your life away on the American dream of retirement. You are as secure as Christ is righteous and God is just. Don't settle for anything less than the joyful sorrows of magnifying Christ in the sacrifices of love.[14]

Dress Rehearsal

If I were to capture the essence of this book, it would be that we are participating in a grand dress rehearsal prior to the wedding of the ages. As followers of Christ, we are preparing for the return of Christ—he the bridegroom and we, the church, his beloved bride (described in Isaiah 62):

> As a young man marries a young woman,
> so will your Builder marry you;
> as a bridegroom rejoices over his bride,
> so will your God rejoice over you. (Isaiah 62:5)

As we have learned and put into practice what it means to be clothed in Christ, we are essentially readying ourselves for the day and moment when we walk the aisle of heaven to meet the Lover of our souls. The wedding itself—the union of our spiritual bodies with Christ's—is described best in the book of Revelation:

CLOTHED with CHRIST

> Let us rejoice and be glad give him glory!
> For the wedding of the Lamb has come,
> and his bride has made herself ready.
> Fine linen, bright and clean,
> was given her to wear. (Revelation 19:7–8)

> I saw the Holy City, the new Jerusalem, coming down out of heaven from God, prepared as a bride beautifully dressed for her husband. And I heard a loud voice from the throne saying, "Look! God's dwelling place is now among the people, and he will dwell with them. They will be his people, and God himself will be with them and be their God. 'He will wipe every tear from their eyes. There will be no more death' or mourning or crying or pain, for the old order of things has passed away.... One of the seven angels who had the seven bowls full of the seven last plagues came and said to me, "Come, I will show you the bride, the wife of the Lamb." And he carried me away in the Spirit to a mountain great and high, and showed me the Holy City, Jerusalem, coming down out of heaven from God. It shone with the glory of God, and its brilliance was like that of a very precious jewel, like a jasper, clear as crystal. (Revelation 21:2–4, 9–11)

The book of Matthew (25:1–13) describes a story Jesus told about ten virgins who were charged with lighting the way of a bridegroom arriving prior to his wedding. Five of the virgins were wise, while the other five were foolish. The wise virgins took with them lamps filled with oil, while the foolish virgins took lamps without oil. The bridegroom was late in arriving and so, the ten virgins naturally fell asleep.

"At midnight the cry rang out: 'Here's the bridegroom! Come out to meet him!'"

"Then all the virgins woke up and trimmed their lamps. The foolish ones said to the wise, 'Give us some of your oil; our lamps are going out.'"

In Your Glad Rags

"'No,' they replied, 'there may not be enough for both us and you. Instead, go to those who sell oil and buy some for yourselves.'

"But while they were on their way to buy the oil, the bridegroom arrived. The virgins who were ready went in with him to the wedding banquet. And the door was shut.

"Later the others also came. 'Lord, Lord,' they said, 'open the door for us!'

"But he replied, 'Truly I tell you, I don't know you.'

"Therefore keep watch, because you do not know the day or the hour [he may arrive.]"

The underlying premise of this story is that we should always be prepared or dressed for when our bridegroom returns. "Look, I come like a thief!" says Jesus (Revelation 16:15). "Blessed is the one who stays awake and remains clothed, so as not to go naked and be shamefully exposed." If we have taken seriously the call to be "clothed with Christ," then we can greet our Lord on that day, clothed in his righteousness, with the confidence and full assurance that we have made every attempt to follow in his footsteps and have intentionally engaged in our own spiritual transformation.

Dallas Willard in *The Great Omission* describes a "golden triangle" of spiritual transformation that involves three essential aspects of putting on Christ:

- Faithful acceptance of everyday problems through which God's character is developed in our lives.

- Interaction with God's Spirit within and around us, manifested through spiritual gifts and by the fruits of the Spirit.

- Practice of spiritual disciplines such as solitude and study, prayer and reflection, service and secrecy, fasting and worship.[15]

"The single most obvious trait of those who profess Christ but do not grow into Christ-likeness," says Willard, "is their refusal to take the reasonable and time-tested measures for spiritual growth."[16] As such, they have failed to clothe themselves with Christ. Their name badge may say "Christian," but they are otherwise either naked or dressed in shabby, threadbare, ill-fitting, or showy coverings that bear little or no resemblance to the Author and Giver of life.

Red Carpet Christians

Imagine if our spiritual attire truly embodied Christ's attributes and qualities. What if, like Hollywood celebrities arriving to a gala event and walking the red carpet, our arrival was announced in similar fashion?

> Reporter 1: And now arriving in a beautiful robe of righteousness and adorned with several fruits of the Spirit, Jennifer McCarthy looks glorious in a dress that truly reflects the unique design of its Creator. Wouldn't you agree, Stephanie?
>
> Reporter 2: Indeed it does, Melissa. And Jennifer is escorted by her husband of thirty-some years, Kent, who looks regal in his fashionable suit accessorized stylishly with Truth and Peace. Oh, and behind them is Brian Stevens, who is sporting a snappy outfit that bears the imprint of the Messiah. You just can't miss that extra attention to detail that shouts, "Glory to God."
>
> Reporter 1: Oh yes, Brian's taste in clothing speaks volumes as to where his heart is and—wait—is that who I think it is stepping out of the black limo? Oh, my goodness, it is! It's Vanessa Applebee wearing a dazzling white ensemble that leaves no doubts about her future destination.
>
> Reporter 2: It certainly is amazing to see all of these shining stars here tonight, Melissa. I'm reminded of the Apostle

In Your Glad Rags

Paul's words about shining like stars in the sky in the midst of a crooked generation.

Reporter 1: Yes, Stephanie. Everyone is certainly decked out in God's finest tonight and making the effort to be clothed with Christ in every sense of word.

Report 2: Amen to that, Melissa.

Cut From the Same Cloth

Our journey together over the past several pages is nearing its end, although the real journey continues for all of us as long as we remain on this earth. My prayer is that you now have a better understanding and awareness of your Christly dress and how it is to be displayed for the world to see. "Let your light shine before others, that they may see your good deeds and glorify your Father in heaven," Jesus reminds us. Put a different way, let your spiritual clothing reflect Christ's character and qualities so that much is made of God in the end. Allow him to tailor your divine attire, for if we are truly "cut from the same cloth" as our Lord Jesus, then our spiritual garb will mirror his image and glory.

I encourage you to go back and reflect on specific chapters and the life application questions that followed. Then purposely form a specific plan as to how you will act on your intentions. Above all, make prayer a priority as you seek to "dress the part" of a follower of Christ. Evaluate your wardrobe and decide: What no longer fits, what is outdated, what is clearly worldly vs. Kingdom garb. Then contemplate and ask God to clothe you with qualities that Jesus exuded. Pray to be clothed with his compassion, kindness, humility, gentleness, patience, and love. Pray to be outfitted with the fruits of the Spirit—love, joy, peace, patience, kindness, goodness, faithfulness, gentleness, and self-control. Pray to be suited in the armor of God. And when not knowing how to pray or what to ask for, consider using the following prayer which I often use to start my day:

CLOTHED with CHRIST

Lord Jesus,
Clothe me with your mind and wisdom to think of things above and to discern your will.
Clothe me with your eyes to notice those who are broken and needy.
Clothe me with your ears to hear and respond to the pleas of those who are hurting.
Clothe me with your mouth to speak words of grace, peace, and encouragement.
Clothe me with your back to shoulder the burdens of others and help carry their load.
Clothe me with your arms to embrace those who are unloved, grieving, and marginalized.
Clothe me with your hands to serve the poor and disadvantaged.
Clothe me with your legs and feet to carry the Gospel to those who need to receive God's grace.
Clothe me with your heart to love unconditionally as the Father loves.
Amen***

I suspect that for every professing believer who is useless in this world because of other-worldliness, there are a hundred who are useless because of this-worldliness. (John Piper)

If you read history, you will find that the Christians who did most for the present world were just those who thought most of the next.... It is since Christians have largely ceased to think of the other world that they have become so ineffective in this. Aim at Heaven and you will get earth "thrown in"; aim at earth and you will get neither. (C. S. Lewis, Mere Christianity)

Someday you will read or hear that Billy Graham is dead. Don't you believe a word of it. I shall be more alive than I am now. I will just have changed my address. I will have gone into the presence of God. (Billy Graham)

In Your Glad Rags

*The etymology of the expression *dressed to the nines* seems largely unknown or speculative. One origin suggests that nine yards of material were needed to make a really nice suit. Another clothing origin suggests that the phrase descended from the Old English saying "dressed to the eyes," which was written as "dressed to thine eynes," which eventually became misinterpreted as "the nines." The number *nine* itself has biblical significance as being thought of as the number of perfection or divine completeness, judgment, or finality. Many have noted the connection to the *nine* fruits of the Spirit or that Jesus died in the *ninth* hour.[17]

**The origin of the word "retirement" comes from the French word for retreat or to withdraw from to a place of safety or seclusion.

***A similar prayer attributed to St. Patrick also captures the spirit of being clothed with Christ:

> *Christ with me, Christ before me, Christ behind me,*
> *Christ in me, Christ beneath me, Christ above me,*
> *Christ on my right, Christ on my left,*
> *Christ when I lie down, Christ when I sit down,*
> *Christ in the heart of everyone who thinks of me,*
> *Christ in the mouth of everyone who speaks of me,*
> *Christ in the eye that sees me,*
> *Christ in the ear that hears me.*

A(fter)word of Encouragement

It's been said that everyone has a book inside waiting to be written. If that's the case, this book seemed to be *begging* to be written. The fact that I did not initially or intentionally set out to put down my thoughts in printed form speaks much of the work God has been doing in my heart for several years and the influence of the Holy Spirit in my reading, pondering, and writing. Likewise, if I had known that I would try to capture my thoughts into something that other people might read, I might have balked and never put pen to paper (or fingers to keyboard).

I mean, who am I, and why would I have anything to say about spiritual transformation? And why would anyone want to hear what I have to say when there are so many other experts and theologians who can speak volumes on the topic? I then realized that that is what the Enemy wants me to think because to speak and write and breathe life into this crazy, mixed-up world is antithetical to his game plan. Andrew Peterson, in his book *Adorning the Dark*, put it this way:

> One holy way of mending the world is to sing, to write, to paint, to weave *new* worlds. Because the seed of your feeble-yet-faithful work fell to the ground, died, and rose again, what Christ has done through you will call forth praise from lonesome travelers long after your name is forgotten. They will know someone lived and loved here. . . . That is why the Enemy wants you to think you have no song to write, no story to tell, no painting to paint. He wants to quiet you. So *sing*. Let the Word by which the Creator made you fill your imagination, guide your pen, lead you from note to note until a melody is strung together like a glimmering constellation in the clear sky. Love the Lord your God, and love your neighbor, too, by making worlds and works of beauty that blanket the earth like flowers.[1]

If this resonates with you, then by all means, go write the book, the script, the blog, the song or poem—whatever the Spirit of creativity has placed on your heart and in your mind, go for it! Nothing ventured, nothing gained. Carpe diem. Go for broke. Whatever maxim gives you the courage and tenacity to see your dream come to fruition, make it yours. And whether or not it sees the light of day or graces the pages of *Publisher's Weekly*, at least you took the first step beyond self-doubt and fear of failure.

If you still need some encouragement, consider the story of Mark Batterson, author and pastor of the National Community Church in Washington, D.C., who has written several best-selling books. Yet getting that first book into print wasn't easy for him. In his book *If: Trading Your If Only Regrets for God's What If Possibilities*, Batterson speaks of making a vow—a bold prediction—that he would write a book by his thirty-fifth birthday.[2] But having made that vow as a twenty-two-year-old seminary student, he saw birthdays come and go with no result. Finally, a mere forty days before he turned the big 3-5, Batterson made the pledge that he would not celebrate that birthday without a published book in hand. He finally fulfilled his vow with the printing of his first book, *ID: The True You*—this after taking an occupational assessment that indicated he had a low aptitude for writing. But Batterson overcame this challenge and responded to God's call by doing his due diligence. Realizing that he couldn't make bold predictions and then expect things to fall in his lap, he "fanned into flame the gift of God" by absorbing thousands of books and honing his craft through countless sermon manuscripts and blog posts. Now at age fifty, Batterson has eighteen books to his credit.

Many feel called to write but are stifled by their perceived lack of talent or otherwise. Excuses become the fodder for an unfinished book or project. I'm too young, you say. Yet Christopher Paolini wrote and published his fantasy book, *Eragon*, in his teens. Too old? Margaret Ford became the world's oldest debut author after publishing her first book at the age of 93. What if my writing is rejected? J. K. Rowling, author of the best-selling *Harry Potter* series, was rejected at least twelve times by major publishers, and Dr. Seuss had his first book rejected twenty-seven times. No formal education

A(fter)word of Encouragement

or training? Mark Twain and Charles Dickens were both forced to end their formal education at the age of twelve.

If you feel that God has given you a message to share, a story to encourage, a lesson to be learned, or a song to inspire, keeping it to yourself may border on disobedience, or at the very least, display a lack of trust in God's design and purpose for you. "You are the light of the world," Jesus said. "A town built on a hill cannot be hidden. Neither do people light a lamp and put it under a bowl. Instead they put it on its stand, and it gives light to everyone in the house. In the same way, let your light shine before others, that they may see your good deeds and glorify your Father in heaven." (Matthew 5:14–16)

What light are you hiding? Is there someone somewhere who needs to hear your story or song to uplift them—to inspire them to reach their God-given potential? Whether it's a blog, a book, or even something as simple as an email or thank you note, do the thing that God has created you to do. Make him known and show those within your reach that God is busy through his people.

> There has never been the slightest doubt in my mind that the God who started this great work in you would keep at it and bring it to a flourishing finish on the very day Christ Jesus appears. (Philippians 1:6, MSG)
>
> So here's my question: what is your unpainted canvas or unwritten book? What God-given dream is collecting dust? What God-ordained passion remains caged? (Mark Batterson)

Acknowledgments

There are a few people to whom I owe a debt of gratitude for their encouragement and feedback during the writing of this book. First and foremost, I give thanks and glory to God the Father who inspired me to pursue the theme of "Clothed with Christ" on my own. Thank you, Jesus, for being my Lord and Savior and for providing to all of us the model of a humble servant. The Holy Spirit further anointed this endeavor by giving me the words, the metaphors, the references, and the scripture verses to support the concept for this book. Soli Deo Gloria.

Two people specifically gave of their time and encouraging feedback to make sure this author was not just blowing steam but had something life-giving to share. My sister, Beth Grotteland, who is a terrific writer on her own, offered not just her English teacher, red-pen-in-hand comments but also her honest criticism where my manuscript came in a little clunky or was too heady. Thanks, sister, for being my biggest cheerleader and for keeping my manuscript grounded. I know there is a book in you somewhere, waiting to come out.

To my good friend Dr. David Smith, a brother in Christ, who made the very kind decision to read over my manuscript with the analytical eyes of a trained psychologist and the loving heart of a spiritual brother. The time you invested in scrutinizing my writing for misplaced commas, mixed metaphors, and theological accuracy says much about our friendship, but more so, your integrity as a man of God.

There is no question that I am at this place in my life because of two loving parents who "raised up a child in the way he should go." To my parents, Eldon and Joan Bentley—you taught me much about a loving Father, even more so in your actions than in your words. I love you both for all you have done for me and for leading me to Jesus at a young age.

To my family—my wife Susan, daughters Laura and Ellen, and son-in-law Vince, who spurred me on with comments of "How's that book coming, Dad?" I love you all and pray that I continue to be the husband and father God has ordained me to be, flaws and all.

To John Bollinger and Steve Taylor: two men from my church who came into my life three years ago and who joined me on a spiritual journey of a year and a half that left us all transformed and at a better place in our faith. Our triad was the proving ground for many of the ideas presented in this book. "As iron sharpens iron, so one person sharpens another" (Proverbs 27:17).

And finally, to Tom Freiling at VIDE Press, who believed in the concept of my book and saw its potential to uplift and encourage readers in their spiritual transformation.

Notes

Introduction

1. J. D. Meier, "Schotoma: Why You Can't See What's Right in Front of You," *Sources of Insight*, 18 October 2014, www.sourcesofinsight.com/schotoma-why-you-cant-see-whats-right-in-front-of-you/.

2. Eugene H. Peterson, *Eat This Book* (Grand Rapids, MI: Eerdmans, 2006), 20–21.

Chapter 1: Muddy People

1. "Dem Bones Gonna Rise Again Chords and Lyrics," The Traditional Music Library, www.traditionalmusic.co.uk/american-traditional-chords/dem_bones_gonna_rise_again.htm.

2. C. S. Lewis, *The Weight of Glory* (San Francisco: HarperCollins, 2001), 25–26.

3. "The Touch of the Master's Hand," *All Poetry*, allpoetry.com/Myra-Brooks-Welch.

4. Derek Prince, *Secrets of a Prayer Warrior* (Grand Rapids, MI: Chosen Books, 2009), 147.

5. "The Cracked Pot," *Life Charger*, 8 July 2017, lifecharger.org/the-cracked-pot-story/.

6. "Fingerprints of God," *Lyrics.com*, STANDS4 LLC, 2020, Web, 18 May 2020. www.lyrics.com/lyric/27592265/Steven+Curtis+Chapman.

7. Joyce Meyer, *Starting Your Day Right: Devotions for Each Morning of the Year* (New York, NY: Warner Books, Inc, 2003), May 10.

Chapter 2: Nothing to Wear

1. "Humiliating' *Sex Tape* Sex Scenes." *E!Online*, 30 June 2014, www.eonline.com/ca/news/555815/cameron-diaz-and-jason-segel-talk-ridiculous-humiliating-sex-tape-sex-scenes.

2. Lim Min Zang, "Making Friends While Naked and Afraid," *The Straits Times*, 17 June 2015, www.straitstimes.com/lifestyle/entertainment/making-friends-while-naked-and-afraid.

3. Rodney Ho, "Snellville resident on Discovery's 'Naked and Afraid' April 20," *AJC: The Atlanta Journal-Consitution*, 17 April 2014, https://www.ajc.com/blog/radiotvtalk/snellville-resident-discovery-naked-and-afraid-april/LNgQZH07ZpS2OToojKf2FK/.

4. Sounak Mukhopadhyay, "Dating Naked: VH1 Reality Show Asks Contestants Date Without Clothes," *International Business Times*, 31 July 2014, https://www.ibtimes.com.au/dating-naked-vh1-reality-show-asks-contestants-date-without-clothes-1349134.

5. Don Carson, *The God Who Is There: Finding Your Place in God's Story* (Grand Rapids, MI: Baker Books, 2010), 25.

6. John Piper, *This Momentary Marriage: A Parable of Permanence* (Wheaton, IL: Crossway, 2009), 37–38.

7. Tony Rienke, "What We Learn from Nude Reality TV," *Desiring God*, 9 August 2014, www.desiringgod.org/articles/what-we-learn-from-nude-reality-tv.

8. John Piper, "Nudity in Drama and the Clothing of Christ," *Desiring God*, 20 November 2006, https://www.desiringgod.org/articles/nudity-in-drama-and-the-clothing-of-christ.

9. Rienke, op. cit.

10. John White, *The Fight* (Downers Grove, IL: InterVarsity Press, 1976), 84.

Notes

11. Mark Batterson, *Wild Goose Chase* (Colorado Springs, CO: Multnomah Books, 2008), 95.
12. John White, *The Fight* (Downers Grove, IL: InterVarsity Press, 1976), 85.
13. Ibid., 85–86.
14. Brennan Manning, *The Ragamuffin Gospel* (Sisters, OR: Multnomah, 2005), 117.
15. Curt Thompson, "How Neuroscience—and the Bible—Explain Shame," *Christianity Today*, 23 June 2016, www.christianitytoday.com/ct/2016/julaug/how-neuroscience-and-bible-explain-shame.html.
16. Ibid.
17. Ibid.
18. Marilyn Meberg, *Tell Me Everything* (Nashville, TN: Thomas Nelson, 2010), 106.
19. Mark Buchanan, *The Rest of God* (Nashville, TN: W Publishing Group, 2006), 191.

Chapter 3: Clothes Make the Man

1. Jordan Gaines Lewis, "Clothes Make the Man—Literally," *Psychology Today*, 24 August 2012, www.psychologytoday.com/blog/brain-babble/201208/clothes-make-the-man-literally.
2. Ibid.
3. Ibid.
4. Henri Duvernois, "Clothes Make the Man," *More Twists: 18 More Tales that Take a Surprising Turn*, by Burton Goodman (Lincolnwood, IL: Jamestown Publishers, 1993), 112–114.
5. Mark Daniels, "Clothes Makes the Person," 5 November 2006, markdaniels.blogspot.com/2006/11/clothes-makes-person.html.

6. Ibid.
7. C. S. Lewis, *Mere Christianity* (New York: Macmillan, 1952), 161.
8. Lauren Winner, *Wearing God* (San Francisco: Harper One, 2015), 36.
9. Ibid., 44.
10. Ibid., 45.
11. "Ten Questions with Sam Wyche," *Fox Sports*, 4 November 2013, www.foxsports.com/nfl/story/sam-wyche-remains-entertaining-and-opinionated-110413.
12. David Faust, "Anthony Munoz: Eyes on the Goal," *The Lookout*, 3 February 2017, lookoutmag.com/2017/anthony-munoz-eyes-on-the-goal/.
13. "Clothed in Christ," *Adult Sabbath School Bible Study Guide* (Lesson 13, June 2011), absg.adventist.org/pdf.php?file=2011:2Q:SE:PDFs:EAQ211_13.pdf.

Chapter 4: I Wouldn't Be Caught Dead in That

1. Susan Soper, "Mr. Blackwell's Best and Worst," *Legacy.com*, 20 October 2013, www.legacy.com/news/celebrity-deaths/article/mr-blackwells-best-and-worst.
2. Ibid.
3. Martin Douglas, "Mr. Blackwell, Fashion Critic, Dies at 86," *The New York Times*, 21 October 2008, www.nytimes.com/2008/10/21/fashion/21blackwell.html.
4. Ibid.
5. Jeremy Poling, "I Have a Body on My Back," *Sermon Central*, 31 December 2007, www.sermoncentral.com/sermons/i-have-a-body-on-my-back-jeremy-poling-sermon-on-sin-bondage-to-116493.

Notes

6. Jerry Bridges, *Discipline of Grace* (Colorado Springs, CO: NavPress, 1994), 84–85.

7. Charles Duhigg, *The Power of Habit: Why We Do What We Do in Life and Business* (New York: Random House, 2012), 20–25.

8. "Clothed in Christ," *Adult Sabbath School Bible Study Guide* (Lesson 13, June 2011), absg.adventist.org/pdf.php?file=2011:2Q:SE:PDFs:EAQ211_13.pdf.

Chapter 5: A Wolf in Sheep's Clothing

1. *The Phrase Finder*, www.phrases.org.uk/meanings/wolf-in-sheeps-clothing.html.

2. Brennan Manning, *The Ragamuffin Gospel* (Sisters, OR: Multnomah, 2005), 127.

3. Mark Buchanan, *Hidden in Plain Sight* (Nashville: Thomas Nelson, 2007), 88.

4. Kyle Idleman, *Not a Fan* (Grand Rapids: Zondervan, 2011), 73.

5. Ibid., 74.

6. Ibid., 83.

7. Ben Witherington, "The Peter Principle—Part 7," *Patheos*, 11 January 2020, www.patheos.com/blogs/bibleandculture/2020/01/11/the-peter-principle-part-seven/.

8. Manning, op. cit., 135.

9. J. I. Packer, *Your Father Loves You*, Harold Shaw Publishers, 1986, 9/19—see more at: http://deliveredbygrace.com/#sthash.iu8Z1cQU.dpuf

10. Henry G. Bosch, "The Shepherd's Voice," *Gracestoration* (Lesson 10, Bell Sheep), www.gracestoration.org/images/10_Bell_Sheep.pdf.

11. Dallas Willard, *Hearing God* (Downers Grove, IL: InterVarsity Press, 1999), 197.

12. Dallas Willard, *Knowing Christ Today* (New York: HarperOne, 2009), 46.
13. Willard, *Hearing God*, op. cit., 153.
14. Manning, op. cit., 136.
15. Brennan Manning, *Brainy Quote*. www.brainyquote.com/quotes/brennan_manning_531776.

Chapter 6: Fashion: In One Year and Out the Other

1. Elliot Clark, "5 Ways to be a 'Third-Culture' Christian," *The Gospel Coalition*, 18 February 2016, www.thegospelcoalition.org/article/5-ways-to-be-a-third-culture-christian.
2. Ibid.
3. "This California Church Serves Beer During Services," *Relevant*, 3 August 2018, relevantmagazine.com/culture/this-california-church-serves-beer-during-services/.
4. Peter Ditzel, *Word of His Grace*, 11 May 2015, www.wordofhisgrace.org/1cor9_22qa.htm.
5. Clark, op. cit.
6. Daniel Threlfall, "Culture: It's More (or Less) Than You Thought," *Sharefaith*, August 2011, www.sharefaith.com/blog/2011/08/culture-or-less-thought/.
7. Stephen Kirk, *Multiply: Embracing a Life of Grace, Community, and Mission* (Self-Published, 2016), 89.
8. Ruth Malhotra, "Andy Stanley: Christians Are Now the Minority, Must Adapt Approach to Sharing Gospel," *The Christian Post*, 20 March 2013, www.christianpost.com/news/andy-stanley-christians-are-now-the-minority-must-adapt-approach-to-sharing-gospel-92232/.
9. Doug Pollock, *God Space: Where Spiritual Conversations Happen Naturally* (Loveland, CO: Group Publishing, 2009), 58.

Notes

10. Kirk, op. cit., 90.
11. Ibid., 90.
12. Ibid., 90.
13. Pollock, op. cit., 13.
14. Mark Batterson, *Wild Goose Chase* (Colorado Springs, CO: Multnomah Books, 2008), 150.
15. John Piper, "Becoming All Things to All Men to Save Some," *Desiring God*, 18 February 1996, https://www.desiringgod.org/messages/becoming-all-things-to-all-men-to-save-some.
16. Kirk, op. cit., 91.
17. James Emery White, "How Much Do You Have to Hate Someone?" *Church and Culture*, 11 February 2019, www.churchandculture.org/blog/2019/2/11/how-much-do-you-have-to-hate-someone.
18. Pollock, op. cit., 67.
19. Ibid., 69.
20. Richard Clark, host, "Lee Strobel's Hope for Apologetics in a 'Post-Truth' Culture," *The Calling, Christianity Today*, 5 April 2015, www.christianitytoday.com/ct/2017/april-web-only/lee-strobels-hope-for-apologetics-in-post-truth-culture.html.
21. Jason D. Bradley, "Should We Still Be Looking for Ways to 'Prove' the Bible?" *Relevant*, 8 August 2017, relevantmagazine.com/article/should-we-still-be-looking-for-ways-to-prove-the-bible/.
22. Kirk, op. cit., 92.
23. Ibid., 92–93.

Chapter 7: Dressed for Battle—Part 1

1. "GDFB 2003 re-enactment shop for all periods from Greek to Late Medieval," *Get Dressed for Battle*, www.gdfb.co.uk/.

2. John White, *The Fight* (Downers Grove, IL: InterVarsity Press, 1976), 216.

3. Kay Arthur, *Lord, Is It Warfare?* (Sisters, OR: Multnomah Books, 1991), 167–168.

4. Rick Renner, *Dressed to Kill* (Tulsa, OK: Teach All Nations Publishing, 2007), 181–184.

5. Scott Bayles, "Holy Heroes: Iron-Man," *Sermon Central*, 3 January 2014, www.sermoncentral.com/sermons/holy-heroes-iron-man-scott-bayles-sermon-on-armor-of-god-181766?page=1.

6. T. D. Jakes, *Overcoming the Enemy* (Bloomington, MN: Bethany House, 2000), 76.

7. Tom Papez, "Batman's Belt," *Sermon Central*, 13 April 2012, www.sermoncentral.com/sermons/batmans-belt-tom-papez-sermon-on-truth-166122?page=1

8. Priscilla Shirer, *The Armor of God* (Nashville, TN: Lifeway Press, 2015), 40.

9. Ibid., 47–50.

10. Kevin J. Vanhoozer, "Core Exercises: How Focusing on our Theological Center Helps Us Remember Who We Are," *Christianity Today*, November 2018, 50.

11. Rick Renner, *Dressed to Kill* (Tulsa, OK: Teach All Nations Publishing, 2007), 264.

12. Ibid., 271.

13. Arthur, op. cit., 183.

14. Renner, op. cit., 276.

15. Shirer, op. cit., 44.

16. Renner, op. cit., 293.

17. Ibid., 294.

Notes

18. Shirer, op. cit., 71.
19. Henry Blackaby, *Experiencing God* (Nashville, TN: Lifeway Press, 1990), 20.
20. Bill Bright, "Experiencing the Adventure," *Cru*, www.cru.org/train-and-grow/transferable-concepts/walk-in-the-spirit.html.
21. "Terrorist," *Lexico*, 2020, en.oxforddictionaries.com/definition/terrorist.
22. "Hijack," *Lexico*, 2020, en.oxforddictionaries.com/definition/us/hijack.
23. "Disarming Cognitive Distortions with Biblical Truth," *Heritage Counseling Center*, 11 March 2015, heritagecounselingcenter.blogspot.com/2015/03/disarming-cognitive-distortions-with.html.

Chapter 8: Dressed for Battle—Part 2

1. Kay Arthur, *Lord, Is It Warfare?* (Nashville, TN: Lifeway Press, 2015), 207.
2. Rick Renner, *Dressed to Kill* (Tulsa, OK: Teach All Nations Publishing, 2007), 314.
3. Ibid., 315.
4. Ibid., 322.
5. Priscilla Shirer, *The Armor of God* (Nashville, TN: Lifeway Press, 2015), 115.
6. Ibid., 127.
7. Ibid., 135.
8. Ibid., 139.
9. Tony Evans, *Victory in Spiritual Warfare*, (Eugene OR: Harvest House Publishers, 2011), 95.
10. Shirer, op. cit., 140.

11. Renner, op. cit., 375–376.
12. Ibid., 377.
13. Shirer, op. cit., 168.
14. Rick Warren, "The Battle for Your Mind," *Desiring God*, 1 October 2010, www.desiringgod.org/messages/the-battle-for-your-mind.
15. Shirer, op. cit., 155.
16. Renner, op. cit., 394.
17. Ibid., 407.
18. Ibid., 415.
19. Ibid., 430.
20. Rick Renner, "The Lance of Prayer and Supplication," *Renner: Teaching You Can Trust*, 2 December 2016, renner.org/the-lance-of-prayer-and-supplication/.
21. John White, *The Fight* (Downers Grove, IL: InterVarsity Press, 1976), 217.
22. Atul Gawande, *The Checklist Manifesto* (New York: Metropolitan Books, 2009).
23. Shirer, op. cit., 15.
24. "Pray on the Armor of God," *Navigators*, www.navigators.org/resource/pray-armor-god/?APCode=E294&gclid=EAIaIQobChMI_fbYvKGc2gIVhSSBCh0s6QvcEAMYAyAAEgJv

Chapter 9: In Your Glad Rags

1. "Clothed in Christ," *Adult Sabbath School Bible Study Guide* (Lesson 13, June 2011), absg.adventist.org/assets/public/files/lessons/2011/2Q/TE/PDFs/ETQ211_11.pdf.
2. Ibid., absg.adventist.org/assets/public/files/lessons/2011/2Q/TE/PDFs/ETQ211_13.pdf.

Notes

3. "Mahalia Jackson: The Queen of Gospel," 2020, www.mahaliajackson.us/.
4. Brad Andres, "Don't Be So Heavenly Minded That You're No Earthly Good," *Brad Andre.com.*, 10 April 2017, www.bradandres.com/dont-be-so-heavenly-minded-that-youre-no-earthly-good/.
5. Ibid.
6. Quoted in Jeff Haanen, "Saving Retirement," *Christianity Today*, March 2019, 39.
7. Rex Rutkoski, "Remembering Billy Graham: 'I'm not going to retire until God retires me,'" *Trib Live*, 22 February, 2018, triblive.com/lifestyles/morelifestyles/13335559-74/remembering-billy-graham-im-not-going-to-retire-until-god-retires-me.
8. John Piper, "Don't Waste Your Life," *Desiring God*, 19 May 2017, www.desiringgod.org/messages/boasting-only-in-the-cross/excerpts/dont-waste-your-life.
9. "Live Like You Were Dying," *Lyrics.com*. STANDS4 LLC, 2020, Web, 18 May 2020, https://www.lyrics.com/lyric/8685327/Tim+McGraw.
10. Chuck Swindoll quoted in Stephen Arterburn and Fred Stoeker, *Every Woman's Desire* (Colorado Springs, CO: Water Brook Press, 2001), 156.
11. Bob Buford, *Halftime: Changing Your Game Plan from Success to Significance*, EPUB, Zondervan, 2015.
12. Jeff Haanen, "Saving Retirement," *Christianity Today*, March 2019, 40.
13. Ibid., 40–41.
14. John Piper, *Rethinking Retirement: Finishing Life for the Glory of Christ* (Wheaton, IL: Crossway Books, 2008), 25–29.

15. Dallas Willard, *The Great Omission* (New York: HarperOne, 2006), 26–28.

16. Ibid., 30.

17. Matt Soniak, "Where Did the Phrase 'Dressed to the Nines' Come From?" *Mental Floss*, 8 April 2013, https://www.mentalfloss.com/article/49785/where-did-phrase-%E2%80%9Cdressed-nines%E2%80%9D-come.

A(fter)word of Encouragement

1. Andrew Peterson, *Adorning the Dark* (Nashville: B & H Publishing Group, 2019), 183.

2. Mark Batterson, *If: Trading Your If Only Regrets for God's What if Possibilities* (Grand Rapids, MI: Baker Books, 2015), 205–205.

www.ingramcontent.com/pod-product-compliance
Lightning Source LLC
Chambersburg PA
CBHW021106080526
44587CB00010B/414